JESSICA SWALE

Jessica Swale is a writer and director, and the Artistic Director of Red Handed Theatre Company. She trained at Central School of Speech and Drama and the University of Exeter.

Her first play, *Blue Stockings*, premiered at Shakespeare's Globe and won her a nomination for Most Promising Playwright in the Evening Standard Awards 2013. She is now writing the screenplay, and an original film, *Summerland*, after winning a JJ Screenwriting Bursary from BAFTA. Other plays include *Thomas Tallis* (Shakespeare's Globe); *All's Will That Ends Will* (Bremer Shakespeare Company); adaptations of *Far from the Madding Crowd*, *Sense and Sensibility* (Watermill Theatre); *The Secret Garden* (Grosvenor Park); and a new play, *The Mission*, about illegal adoptions in the 1920s.

Jessica has directed a number of award-winning productions for Red Handed, which is dedicated to creating new work and rediscovering forgotten plays. Recent productions include *The Rivals* starring Celia Imrie, the London premiere of *Palace of the End* by Judith Thompson, and the first major revival of Hannah Cowley's *The Belle's Stratagem*, which won her a nomination for Best Director at the Evening Standard Awards.

Other direction includes *Bedlam* (Shakespeare's Globe); *Sleuth* (Watermill); *Fallen Angels* (Salisbury Playhouse); *Winter* (TNL, Canada); *The Busy Body*, *Someone to Watch Over Me* (Southwark), *The School for Scandal* (Park Theatre); and productions at RADA and LAMDA. Jessica was Max Stafford-Clark's Associate Director at Out of Joint from 2007–2010.

Jessica is an associate artist with Youth Bridge Global, an international NGO which uses theatre as a tool for promoting social change in war-torn and developing nations. As such, she has lived in the Marshall Islands and in Bosnia and Herzegovina, directing Shakespeare productions including *The Comedy of Errors*, *Much Ado About Nothing*, *Twelfth Night* and *The Tempest*.

She has wr............ ....a
Games ser.   nd
for Rehear

D1394108

Other Titles in this Series

Jessica Swale

NELL GWYNN

NICK HERN BOOKS

London

www.nickhernbooks.co.uk

A Nick Hern Book

Nell Gwynn first published in Great Britain as a paperback original in 2015 by Nick Hern Books Limited, The Glasshouse, 49a Goldhawk Road, London W12 8QP

Nell Gwynn copyright © 2015 Jessica Swale

Jessica Swale has asserted her right to be identified as the author of this work

Cover image: Gugu Mbatha-Raw as Nell Gwynn, photograph © 2015 Michael Wharley (www.michaelwharley.com)

Typeset by Nick Hern Books, London
Printed in Great Britain by Mimeo Ltd, Cambridgeshire PE29 6XX

A CIP catalogue record for this book is available from the British Library

ISBN   978 1 84842 494 4

'The People Loved Her Because She Was One of Them'

An Interview with Jessica Swale
Speaking to Heather Neill

Nell Gwynn, orange seller and mistress of Charles II, is a figure of legend, but where did she come from?

It's hard to know exactly; working-class lives weren't recorded in enough detail for there to be accurate records, but many believe she was brought up in Coal Yard Alley in Covent Garden, where her mother, 'Old Ma Gwynn', kept a brothel. Nell probably worked there, either serving drinks to clients or as a prostitute. Some say she worked as a herring gutter or oyster hawker before she began selling oranges in the pit at Drury Lane. Her father died in a debtors' prison and she had one sister called Rose. Part of the joy of writing *Nell Gwynn* has been sketching around the bones of the known facts, imagining and inventing. I never set out to write a documentary-style play, but even if I had, the task would have proved impossible with the inconsistencies and contradictions in her history.

What was the life of an orange seller like?

The girls sold sharp China oranges and sweetmeats in baskets, whilst earning tips passing messages between punters and backstage like a seventeenth-century Tinder. Many were prostitutes too. It's not clear how Nell got onstage, but I like to imagine that she was spotted wittily doing her job by Charles Hart.

Hart was the star of the day.

Yes and she did become his mistress. Dryden wrote plays for them both in Thomas Killigrew's company. Nell was a highly successful and popular comic actress and, although she was illiterate, it's very likely that she really did invent and perform the Epilogue of our play.

What was theatre like when it was re-established after Cromwell's Commonwealth?

When Charles II returned from France in 1660, he licensed two theatre companies in London: Killigrew's King's Company at Drury Lane and Davenant's Duke's Company at Lincoln's Inn Fields. I imagine Killigrew must have been under tremendous pressure as the two companies were in constant competition. At Drury Lane there was an apron stage and a pit filled with benches rather than standing groundlings. Society was much smaller then, so all classes would meet at the theatre – and the Globe emulates that democratic feel. As for Dryden, it is funny that so many of his plays are badly written, but he must have felt the weight of expectation; theatre was re-emerging after an eleven-year gap, he was at the helm of the new culture, the King wanted new plays – it can't have been easy. No wonder they reinvented so many familiar texts. There was a fashion for rewriting Shakespeare, particularly cheering up the tragedies. *King Lear* was given a new ending in which Cordelia survives, and Dryden wrote a 'new play' called *The Enchanted Island*, about Prospero and his *two* daughters – Miranda and Dorinda. Sound familiar? Yet, though his plays haven't stood the test of time, he was a successful poet and even became Poet Laureate.

How did the first actresses fit into the picture?

Charles II had seen actresses on stage in Paris and decided it was high time we followed fashion. However, the early actresses got a rather raw deal. Writers knew the audiences interest in actresses was often voyeuristic, so played into this by writing body-exposing rape scenes, or writing 'breeches parts', in which women, disguised as tight-trousered men (exposing their shapely legs) were then revealed to be female with the dramatic exposure of their breasts. Punters often paid an extra penny to watch the actresses change, many of whom were prostitutes. This was Nell's world, but I wanted her to question it. If she was learning the craft, falling in love with acting, surely someone of her wit and intelligence would want better parts to play than the 'wilting waifish woman'. She wasn't the first woman on stage; that was probably Margaret Hughes, or possibly (as in this play) Moll Davies at the rival company, but Nell was in the first wave of actresses.

You have had considerable success directing plays of this period. Did you consider writing in the style of a Restoration play?

Whilst I originally considered writing in a Restoration style, I thought it would be alienating (and a little perverse) to use archaic language, to be overly verbose and use magniloquent phraseology unnecessarily (you see). What was far more important to me was to capture the quick wit of the time and the equivalent of that for us is more akin to modern farce. So that's what this is. I've peppered it with period references, but I've chosen to use modern syntax and diction, with the occasional anachronism for comic effect.

You have actors demonstrating 'attitudes', poses to indicate emotions. Would the acting style have seemed alien to us?

It's easy to assume that it was melodramatic, but actually Pepys describes the best actors as seeming real, so I wonder if the style somehow used precise physical positions as a structure, rather like ballet, whilst still being emotionally connected, like naturalism. The 'attitudes' weren't static poses but frameworks of movements and gestures which actors used to underscore the text. As theatres were large buildings, it was important that emotion could be read in an actor's posture. Heightened emotion, stylised, but still real.

Are the songs in the play based on the music of the period?

They're certainly inspired by it. I love writing lyrics, and had been listening to everything from Purcell to an album called *The History of Bawdy Songs*, which tells you all you need to know! So I would write in pastiche of a style, then pass the lyrics on to Nigel Hess, who would transform them by writing original melodies and scoring them so beautifully that they'd become unrecognisable. He is a genius, I think.

How much is known of Nell's relationship with the King?

I think they really were in love. She was his favourite mistress for many years, and they spent a lot of private time together. He had a secret passage built from his court rooms in Westminster to her house in Pall Mall, so they could rendezvous for card games and evenings away from the public. Unlike Barbara Castlemaine, she made no attempt to interfere in politics and never asked for a title for herself (though she did for her sons). Louise de Keroualle, another favourite mistress and Nell's rival, was tremendously unpopular and was known as 'the Catholic whore'. There's a story that a crowd once attacked Nell's coach thinking Louise was inside, so Nell merrily stuck her head out and said 'Hold, good people, I am the *Protestant* whore!' which garnered whoops and cheers from the delighted onlookers. The people loved her because she was one of them. And, of course, there's Charles's famous dying wish: 'Don't let poor Nellie starve.'

Who was Arlington, the courtier?

Arlington was an ambitious advisor to the King, significantly older and more experienced. I've conflated him with Buckingham to give Charles a right-hand man. He may seem outspoken in his manner with the King, but the reality is that the Court was terribly shaken after the Commonwealth, and it was essential that Charles didn't put a foot wrong. The divine right of kings had just been re-established, order restored, the aristocrats returned. If Arlington and his courtiers could ensure the King's image was spotless, divine, he would stay on his pedestal. But if his saintly image was tarnished by an affair with a prostitute from Coal Yard Alley, who would see him as divine then? What would stop the next Cromwell?

One of your themes is celebrity.

It's fascinating to ask whether Nell's celebrity was because of her brilliance as an actress or because she was the King's mistress. Pamphleteers – like paparazzi today – would quickly report the activities of the famous, and Charles (and his mistresses) were the hot topic. There was such a frenzy to see him that they even allowed the public into the gallery to watch him eat dinner at night. There was a culture of writing lewd poems about society figures; just look at Rochester. So if there's a few dirty jokes in the play, don't blame me, it's all in the name of historical accuracy...

Was it difficult to distinguish fact from legend and gossip?

Yes, and I made a decision early on that the play should be an entertaining homage to Nell rather than an attempt at documentary-style historical accuracy. Otherwise the play would be a week long, and have to include the fire of London, the plague and the entire Court decamping to Oxford in 1665, just for starters. I made giant wall charts coursing the events of the theatre and the Court, but even then there are contradictions where historians debate when and how. I have drawn on hearsay; the story of the laxatives, for example. But primarily I wanted to honour Nell's memory, to capture her spirit and what she stood for rather than stick slavishly to facts. The key events of the play are historically accurate, but I've allowed myself to embellish. Primarily, I wanted it to be fun. And if it's a play that Nell would have enjoyed, that's enough for me.

Reprinted with kind permission of Shakespeare's Globe.
Heather Neill is a freelance journalist and theatre historian.

Acknowledgements

A play, as Killigrew would no doubt attest, is nothing without its company of players. Enormous thanks to the Globe company; to Dominic Dromgoole for saying yes, to the cast, crew and creative team, to Nigel Hess for his gorgeously bawdy songs, Huw Durrant for his extraordinary set and costumes, Matt Dann for inexhaustible enthusiasm and most of all to Chris Luscombe, who has the patience of a saint and the sense of humour of a devil, and with whom I have had the greatest adventure.

Thank you to the actors at LAMDA who breathed life into these characters in their infancy, when the script was a Dryden-esque scribble. To Joanna Read, Derek Bond. To Raz Shaw and his cast, Bathsheba Piepe, Adam Scott-Rowley, Daisy Badger, Donal Gallery, Ollo Clark, Raphael Acloque, Sally O'Leary and Toby Gordon. Thank you too to all at RADA, particularly Lloyd Trott, dramaturg extraordinaire. Thank you to our Globe workshop actors – the indefatigable George Banks, Penelope Beaumont, Michael Bryher, Natalie Casey, Jackie Clune, Gerard McCarthy, Dorothea Myers-Bennett and David Newman.

Thank you to Matt Applewhite, Sarah Liisa Wilkinson and all at Nick Hern Books, to Helen Mumby and the team at MLR, to Ella Smith for helping me find my funny bones, to my folks for their constant support and to Michael, for always being there, late-night whisky at the ready.

J.S.

Nell Gwynn was first performed at Shakespeare's Globe, London, on 19 September 2015, with the following cast:

NELL GWYNN	Gugu Mbatha-Raw
ROSE GWYNN	Anneika Rose
NANCY	Amanda Lawrence
LADY CASTLEMAINE/ LOUISE DE KEROUALLE	Sasha Waddell
OLD MA GWYNN/ QUEEN CATHERINE	Sarah Woodward
KING CHARLES II	David Sturzaker
CHARLES HART	Jay Taylor
THOMAS KILLIGREW	Richard Katz
EDWARD KYNASTON	Greg Haiste
JOHN DRYDEN	Graham Butler
LORD ARLINGTON	David Rintoul
NED SPIGGETT	Angus Imrie
Director	Christopher Luscombe
Designer	Hugh Durrant
Composer	Nigel Hess

An earlier version of *Nell Gwynn* was performed by students at LAMDA, as part of the 2014 Long Project, directed by Raz Shaw.

For my three Nells.

For Nell Leyshon. Because that's where it all started.

For Gugu, for making Nell a real woman,
'with skin and heart and some sense in her head'.

And for Nell Gwynn, of course. I owe you one.

Characters

THE LADIES
NELL GWYNN, *our heroine*
ROSE GWYNN, *Nell's sister*
NANCY, *Nell's dresser and confidante*
LADY CASTLEMAINE, *Charles's most ambitious mistress*
LOUISE DE KEROUALLE, *Charles's French mistress*
QUEEN CATHERINE, *Charles's Portuguese wife*
OLD MA GWYNN, *Nell's mother, a brothel madam*

THE GENTS
KING CHARLES II, *the King, obviously*
CHARLES HART, *leading actor in the King's Company*
THOMAS KILLIGREW, *actor-manager of the King's Company*
EDWARD KYNASTON, *actor in the King's Company, plays the women's parts*
JOHN DRYDREN, *playwright*
LORD ARLINGTON, *Charles II's adviser*
NED SPIGGETT, *actor in training in the King's Company*

Other parts are played by members of the company.

The play can be performed with a smaller company when parts are doubled.

Setting

The time is the 1660s. Charles II has ascended the throne. We begin in the playhouse in Drury Lane, London.

Note on the Text

A forward slash (/) denotes overlapping dialogue, where the second speaker begins when the slash appears in the previous person's line.

Note on the Music

The songs in this script form an essential and (I hope) joyous part of *Nell Gwynn*. I wanted the play to celebrate the musicality of the Restoration theatre, which brimmed with song and dance. Most of the lyrics are original, some I have borrow from composers of the era. To get a feel for the genre I'd recommend listening to Purcell for something puritanical, then washing it down with the Baltimore Consort's *The Art of the Bawdy Song* for kicks. Whilst you're free to set the lyrics to music yourselves, I would highly recommend you use Nigel Hess's beautiful song arrangements, which can be licensed from Nick Hern Books.

This text went to press before the end of rehearsals and so may differ slightly from the play as performed.

ACT ONE

Scene One

Prologue

Fanfare. The play is about to begin! The doors open and the young actor NED SPIGGETT *steps out onto the stage to speak the prologue of John Dryden's new play.*

NED. ''Tis said that you, the judges of the town,
  Would pass a vote to put all prologues down.
  For who can show me, since they first were writ,
  They e'er converted one hard-hearted nit.'

  (*Realising his mistake.*) Wit. Wit!

  NED *tries to carry on, but he's thrown. He continues awkwardly.*

  'Yet London's mended well; in former days
  Good prologues were as scarce as now good plays.
  Our poet hopes / you – '

HECKLER 1. Can't hear you!

NED (*a little louder*). 'Our poet hopes you ladies will not find
  His rhyme and prose to be so ill designed.
  Or contemplate that, once the prologue's done;
  The wit is ended...' Um, sorry. (*He's dried.*)
  'The wit...'

HECKLER 2. Oh no.

NED. 'Wit is ended...'

  He subtly checks the lines he has written on his hand.

  ' – Ere the play's begun!'

HECKLER 3. He's got it written on his hand!

HECKLER 1. Cheat!

NELL (*in the audience*). Let him alone! (*To* NED.) I want to hear the play.

NED. Thank you.

Meanwhile, an actor enters surreptitiously, dressed as an astrologer, carrying a telescope, his face covered by his hood.

'So to the heavens must we cast our gaze.'

HECKLER 1. Hey! Blockhead, make us laugh.

NELL (*to the* HECKLER). You want a laugh? Why don't you look in a glass?

HECKLER 1. Enough of your cheek.

NELL. Don't think you've ever seen my cheeks, sir.

HECKLER 1. Everybody else has.

NELL. Every fellow that could afford them, sir. Not you.

NED. Um… shall I carry on?

NELL. Yes, you carry on. (*To the* HECKLER.) Let him play his part. (*To* NED *and the crowd*.) He's just jealous cos no one's played on *his* part for a while.

HECKLER 1. Think you're so quick, don't ya?

NELL. Not as quick as you, sir. So your good wife says.

Laughter from the audience.

NED. Ladies and gentlemen, the lady's a wit!

HECKLER 1. She's an orange hawker! Fool! Close up your hole and have done, woman, we've all had enough of your fruit.

He throws an orange at NED, *which lands on the stage.* NELL GWYNN *decides, against all convention, to walk onto the stage to retrieve it.*

NELL. I am an orange hawker, sir. So thank you for the compliment – and for the return of my stock. But I think you'll find that you are the fool. You paid me a sixpence for this. And now I have it back. So you are left with nowt, while I just doubled my profits.

She puts it back in her basket.

Carry on.

NED. Where was I?

NELL. Gazing at the heavens.

NED. Ah, yes.

> 'So to the heavens must we cast our gaze,
> To peer upon the fortune of our plays.'

He takes a bow. Spooky music. The disguised actor pulls down his hood to reveal CHARLES HART, *the most popular actor of his day. Rapturous applause.*

HART. Ladies and gentlemen. Thank you. And a hand for Miss…

NELL. Gwynn. Nell Gwynn.

HART. Miss Gwynn, thank you for the prologue to the prologue. Now, onwards. What secrets do the heavenly bodies hold?

HART *strikes an attitude and peers through the telescope.*

> 'Aha! First Jupiter o'er Saturn is to reign,
> And in ascendance bears the sign of Spain!
> Whence I conclude, it is our author's lot
> To be endangered by a Spanish plot! (*Boo!*)
> But hold! Now Mars in his apartment rises
> Perchance this English wit may yet surprise us.
> And though he can't the heav'nly bodies steer
> Perhaps his friends on earth may raise a cheer.'

Music. The COMPANY *arrive and burst into song as the play's opening number begins.*

Song – 'A Brimmer to the King'

ALL (*singing*).
> Come boys, fill us a bumper,
> We'll make the nation cheer.
> Bang the drum and the thumper,
> The days of joy are here.

Sing, for London is merry,
Let no man balk his wine,
We'll sink the sack of canary
To toast the King divine.

CHORUS
Fill the pottles and gallons
And bring the hogshead in.
We'll begin with a tallen
And a brimmer to the King!

Into…

Scene Two

The Attitudes

Later that same day, after the performance, NELL *is gathering spilled oranges from the yard.* CHARLES HART *arrives from backstage and calls to her, which takes her by surprise. He is something of a star.*

HART. Gwynn!

NELL. Mr Hart!

HART. What was that?

NELL. Sir?

HART. What exactly did you think you were doing?

NELL. I was just jesting.

HART. Your audacity astounds me.

NELL. Sir, I –

HART. You've got no right to interrupt the prologue.

NELL. I was only trying / to help.

HART. In the middle of Mr Spiggett's performance!

NELL. I didn't mean / to –

HART. You can't just stride up here and talk to him!

NELL. I'm sorry.

HART. Talk to everyone!

Beat.

NELL. What?

HART. Talk to everyone. First rule of acting. Include your audience.

NELL. Sir?

HART. Come along. Put the fruit down and get up here.

NELL. Me?!

HART. Who else?

NELL. But I…

HART. Do you want to learn or not?

NELL. Learn?

HART. Acting.

NELL. But I'm a woman, Mr Hart!

HART. Project. 'Mr Hart!'

NELL. Mr Hart!

Continuing as he helps her onto the stage…

HART (*demonstrating*). Mr Hart!

NELL (*louder*). Mr Hart!

HART (*indicating her diaphragm*). From here!

NELL (*louder*). Mr Hart!

HART (*louder, faster*). Again!

NELL (*louder, faster*). Mr Hart!

HART (*building to a climax*). Say my name!

NELL (*yelling*). Mr Hart!

HART. We'll work on that. Now, being heard is the first lesson. But being felt – conveying the consumptive passions which overwhelm you, as… (*Acts each state out.*) as your lover gasps her final breath. Or elation – as Hymen descends from the heavens. Or the grim sense of callous death which stirs your soul when you spy Old Hamlet's ghost. Try this. 'Terror.'

He pulls a terrified face. She looks at him awkwardly.

Come along!

He pulls the face again. NELL *copies.*

Terror is the first of the attitudes. 'Fear aroused by an object of dismay.' There! Eyebrows raised. Nostrils drawn up. The eyes and mouth are wide. Wide, I say!

She strikes a compelling pose.

Hm. Let's try anger. Fury rises in your bowels. Furrow your forehead. Flare the nostrils and the lips like so.

He demonstrates. She copies.

Now cry out, with all the blood-swelling torment of your heart. Aargh!

NELL. Aargh!

HART (*simultaneously*). Aarrgh!

NELL. AAARGH!

HART. Tolerable. Anger often comes naturally to women.

NELL. Mr Hart!

HART. Well projected. Why don't you try the next one on your own? Despair. 'The absolute privation of hope'; the lost love, the shattered soul. Tears rise, breath catches.

He watches her. She is more naturalistic than one might expect.

Make it bigger. Play it to the gods, they'll never see that at the back. More, Gwynn! Allow it to consume you utterly.

She gives a small look upwards, her eyes filling with tears.

What are you doing? Are you quite all right?

She is on the verge of sobbing.

NELL. I'm – I just –

HART. Nell! I'm sorry. It wasn't a criticism.

NELL *sobs loudly.*

Nell?! Nell!

She drops out of the act immediately.

NELL. I'm just acting, sir.

HART. Well, blow me down, I thought it was real.

NELL. I was only pretending.

HART. But it was convincing. Moving, even. How very intriguing.

NELL. What's next?

HART. Love.

NELL. Love?

HART. Yes, love. 'Pleasant delight with reference to the object of affection.'

NELL (*cheekily*). You mean your lover?

HART. Yes I do. It's the final and most complex of the attitudes. It's not only on the face, but in the very blood. It must possess your entire being.

NELL (*begins to flirt… just a little*). Show me how to do love.

HART (*touching his heart*). It'll be in there.

NELL. Tell me. I'd like to hear it.

HART. Well. Love is 'complete and utter indifference to everything, except the one you admire'.

NELL *follows his instructions with flirtatious confidence; this is one role she knows how to play.* HART*, won over, finds it hard to concentrate.*

Eyebrows raised slightly. Head inclined towards the cause of love. Lips moisten softly with vapours which rise from the heart. Eyes connect with the object of affection.

NELL. I look into your eyes.

HART (*under her spell*). Yes. Yes, you do.

NELL. Might I step towards my 'object of affection'?

HART. Affection, yes. Step towards / your –

NELL. My object of –

HART. Object of affection.

NELL. Desire.

HART. Or – or desire. Yes.

NELL. I'm good, aren't I?

HART (*mesmerised*). You are – surprisingly good.

NELL. 'Love.'

HART. 'Love.'

They both stand close to each other, there is a moment of intensity. A beat. He breaks the spell.

Um, yes. Excellent. Excellent.

NELL. You all right, sir?

HART (*flustered*). What? Yes. No. Exactly.

She looks out over the audience.

You like it up here?

NELL. S'all right.

HART. All right? There's nothing like it, when it's full. Packed in, like pippins on a cart; and all of them, looking at you. It's like no other feeling in the world.

NELL. You *do* like it.

HART. Somehow I've never quite felt myself anywhere else. Which is ironic, now I think of it.

NELL. Odd, though. Pretending for a living.

HART. I suppose it is a strange existence. My father has two dozen scars on his back for his efforts.

NELL. They whipped him?

HART. They said it was 'the devil's work'! But that was before. We're all right for now, as long as Charles keeps his head. So to speak. God save the King, eh?

NELL. If they thought *you* were sinners, lucky they didn't come down the Madam's.

HART. Of course. Sorry.

NELL. Oh, I don't do it any more. Swapped selling my oyster for my oranges, didn't I.

HART. And does it make you happy? Hawking?

NELL. S'pose. I never thought to ask.

Pause.

HART. Listen. If you were willing to work... hard, perhaps I could teach you.

NELL. Teach me?

HART. You would have to commit. Every day, at dusk we'd meet, for a month. And we'd practise. And then, if you show aptitude, I might take you to meet Mr Killigrew. What do you say?

NELL. Why?

HART. Why? I don't quite know.

NELL. I don't think so.

HART. Why not?!

NELL. There's no point.

HART. You don't know that.

NELL. I might not be any good.

HART. Then go back to your oranges.

NELL. And I'm a woman!

HART. What have you got to lose? Say yes.

NELL. Mr Hart.

HART. Say yes!

Pause. Will she? Won't she?

NELL. All right. Yes. Yes!

HART. Good! Well, till tomorrow then!

He goes to leave.

NELL. Sir?

HART. Gwynn?

NELL. Thank you, Mr Hart.

He gives her a look. She projects.

MR HART!

He exits. She watches him go, then tries some poses of her own. She tests her projection, aiming to a different place in the auditorium each time.

Mr Hart! Mr Hart! Mr Hart!

ROSE (*appearing in the yard*). Mr Hart?

NELL. Oh, Rose! I was just… 'Romeo, Romeo!'

ROSE. Come down.

NELL. 'Lend me your ears.'

ROSE. We need to get back.

NELL (*pointing in terror to something behind her*). AARGH!

ROSE (*panicking*). What?!

NELL. Nothing. Just acting. Terror. Eyebrows raised. Nostrils flared.

ROSE. Stop fooling –

NELL. It's a serious art, Rosey. Mr Hart said.

ROSE. Mr Hart? *Charles* Hart?! He spoke to *you*?

NELL *glows a little.*

And what else did Mr Hart say? 'Let's meet again tomorrow'?

NELL. Yep.

ROSE. What? Nell!

NELL. He's teaching me acting.

ROSE. But you're a woman.

NELL. He liked my positions. Said I'm natural.

ROSE. He's an actor!

NELL. So?

ROSE. They're bad types, actors. You can't trust anyone at the playhouse.

NELL. You make your coins here.

ROSE. Doesn't mean I like it. We need your orange money. If you come home without coins, Mother'll / have you.

NELL. He thinks I might be good.

ROSE. You think he gives a sot about your acting? He wants you, Nell.

NELL. You don't know that.

ROSE. He's a man with desires. I know men.

NELL. So do I.

ROSE. Not like I do. You've never had – (*Beat. Can't bring herself to say it.*) You've just been lucky.

NELL. Hey, it's hardly likely to come to anything, but … I want to try. Just in case.

Scene Three

An Actor-ess

A month later. THOMAS KILLIGREW, *the theatre manager, has called a company meeting. So far only* DRYDEN, *the nervy playwright,* NANCY, *the dresser, and* NED *are assembled.* KILLIGREW *is evidently worried.*

KILLIGREW. I suppose you've heard the news.

DRYDEN. What news?

> EDWARD KYNASTON, *who takes the female roles, arrives in a fury.*

KYNASTON. 'What news?!!'

NANCY. Wait for it…

KYNASTON. The crooks! The swindlers! The flaccid bottom-dwelling pig farts!

DRYDEN. What's the matter, Mr Kynaston?

KYNASTON. What's the matter? I'll tell you what's the matter. They've disgraced our trade. Ruined our art.

NED. Who has?

KYNASTON. Ned, sometimes you are as dense as a frozen pail of hog turds. Those muckweeds at the Duke's Company have… they have…

He can't bring himself to say it.

KILLIGREW. They've put a woman on the stage.

NED. A woman?

KYNASTON (*darkly*). A whore.

KILLIGREW. Miss Davies is not a whore. She is an actress.

KYNASTON. A what?

KILLIGREW. An actor-ess.

NANCY. It's a lady actor.

KYNASTON. It's ridiculous, that's what it is. It'll be the death of theatre, I tell you!

DRYDEN. I don't know. We've got women in the company.

KILLIGREW. Nancy washes the stockings and sets the props. She doesn't take the lead.

NANCY. Miss Davies played Desdemona.

KYNASTON. That's my role!

KILLIGREW. And apparently she was rather convincing.

DRYDEN. Did it sell?

KILLIGREW. To the rafters. And now they're queuing all the way to Cheapside.

NANCY. Can you imagine?! We'll be writing plays next.

KYNASTON. Haven't you got laundry to do?

DRYDEN. Perhaps it was just a one-off.

KILLIGREW. Sadly not. They've commissioned a new season, with Moll in the lead. Etheredge is writing it for her.

DRYDEN. Dratting hell, I can't write for a woman!

KYNASTON. You won't need to, darling. Have faith. Audiences have taste.

KILLIGREW. Audiences want entertainment.

KYNASTON. I am entertaining.

KILLIGREW. But you're not Moll Davies.

KYNASTON. And what, pray, does she have that I don't?

NANCY. Tits.

KILLIGREW. Thank you, Nancy.

KYNASTON. Tits! What have tits got to do with it?

KILLIGREW. Unfortunately I think they have rather a lot to do with it.

KYNASTON. That's ridiculous. I have a perfectly rounded, pert pair of linen tits that I am very fond of, thank you. What's the fuss, anyway? It's not like anyone sees them.

There is an awkward pause. KYNASTON *looks to*
KILLIGREW *who looks pained.*

(*Quiet, slow.*) Oh. She doesn't?! Barbarous!

NED. She shows her... ? To the punters?

KILLIGREW. She does.

KYNASTON. And people pay to see that?!

KILLIGREW. Some folk, Mr Kynaston, are rather partial to the
female accoutrements.

KYNASTON. Then they should go to the bawdy house. Theatre
is sophisticated, sublime, not a cheap tattle show where any
old Nancy gets her knockers out.

NANCY. Oy!

KILLIGREW. He didn't mean you, Nancy.

KYNASTON. Desdemona?! It's sacrilege. At what point does
Desdemona get her tits out?

'Good my lord, if I have any power to move you, prithee
come apace and *I'll show you my tits*'?

KILLIGREW. They've done a rewrite, the bit with the pillow –
it's all rather revealing.

DRYDEN. Are there any tickets left?

KILLIGREW. Dryden!

DRYDEN. Sorry.

KILLIGREW. If they start selling out, they'll run us into the
ground. We may have to make... unpopular decisions.

KYNASTON. Is that aimed at anyone in particular?

KILLIGREW. The King has decreed that women should be on
the stage. And he is our patron, don't forget. And who
knows, it might be rather jolly to play a love scene with a
real woman. Imagine. Juliet, a real lady with hopes and
aspirations –

NED. And tits.

KILLIGREW. Yes, Ned – she wouldn't just be convincing. She would be real. Dryden, think! You could write any sort of woman you want – not just the passive lover, the fragile beauty. If you're writing for real women, they won't need to be so feminine any more.

KYNASTON. No, no, no, no, no! You miss the point entirely. Theatre is artifice. It's make-believe. Pretend. The blood is not real blood. Othello's not a real Moor. People come to the playhouse to engage with the imaginary. For a short break from their wretched, drivel-filled lives they can escape. Who'd go to the theatre to see real people saying real things about real life? That would be preposterous! We trade in magic. And we are trained to do it. Honed, groomed, athletes of the imagination. And these women – what training have they had, eh? I want nothing to do with it. The whole thing stinks!

He leaves in a huff and meets HART *in the doorway.*

Oh, Charles, darling, have you heard the news? Everything's going to change.

HART. Yes, yes it is! Gentlemen, the Duke's might have Moll Davies, but wait till you see what I've brought you.

KYNASTON. What – some actor-ess guttersnipe you've found on the streets, ha ha!

NELL *enters.*

Oh Jesus.

HART. Fellows. I'd like you to meet Nell Gwynn.

NED. The orange seller!

HART. This is Mr Dryden, our playwright, Mr Kynaston, our leading lady, Nancy, Ned, and this is Mr Killigrew. (*To* KILLIGREW.) I think you ought to try her out.

KILLIGREW. But she's – (*Hushed.*) she's a strumpet, Charles. No disrespect, ma'am.

NELL. None taken.

HART. Listen. I watched her out there, jesting like a court wit. So we've done a little work together, and, well... I think she has something unusual.

KYNASTON. Syphilis?

KILLIGREW. Miss Gwynn, you do realise acting requires arduous training. They've all trained.

KYNASTON. For years.

KILLIGREW. Not only the attitudes, but the training of / the voice –

KYNASTON. The voice, the breath, the face, the brow, the alignment of the arms, the tripping of the feet –

KILLIGREW. Let's not overwhelm her.

NELL. Mr Hart's taught me the attitudes; I think I know them all.

KYNASTON. Oh really? Which 'all' would that be? All three hundred and seventy-two attitudes according to the Burbage edition of 1661, or the revised copy, with the appendices on twenty-one varieties of grief as expressed by the left eyebrow?

NELL. Oh, I've no need of books, not when you're learning 'by Hart'.

HART *is flattered*. KYNASTON *is disgusted*.

KILLIGREW. Well, why don't we have a little trial. See how you prosper. You see, Miss Gwynn, drama relies on intrigue. What can you communicate to the man you love without your father noticing?

NELL. Or your husband.

NED *laughs*. KILLIGREW *gives him a look*.

HART (*warning*). Nell.

KILLIGREW. A woman is bestowed with one tool with which she can coax a man.

NELL. Oh, I know all about that.

KILLIGREW (*handing her a fan*). I meant your *fan*, Miss Gwynn.

NELL. So did I. My 'fan'. (*Fans herself.*)

KYNASTON. The fan, Mistress Gwynn, is not simply a crass tool for cooling one's brow. To learn the language of the fan is a lifetime's work. You can't just pick it up and wave it on a whim.

KILLIGREW. Let's persevere for a little while, though, shall we?

KYNASTON. It is a complex art. Where did you go to fan school? Oh, you didn't. Exactly!

KILLIGREW. Come, come. Mr Kynaston, perhaps you / could demonstrate.

KYNASTON. I shall demonstrate.

KILLIGREW. Very good.

KYNASTON. Watch.

> KYNASTON, *besotted with* HART, *performs his fan sequence with a jealous intensity to him.*

> (*Hits his palm with his fan.*) Love me. (*Lets his fan go, so it dangles on the wrist ribbon, then gracefully swoops it up.*) I belong to you. (*Touches his cheek with his fan.*) Kiss me on the cheek. (*Places his fan on his heart; to* HART.) My love for you is breaking my heart.

> KYNASTON *runs his fingers through the fan's ribs.*

KILLIGREW. Stroking the ribs.

NED. We need to talk.

> KYNASTON *peers at* HART *over the fan.*

KILLIGREW. Peeping above.

NED. We are being watched.

> KYNASTON *moves the fan to his right and stares at* HART.

KILLIGREW. Placement to the right.

NED. I see that you're looking at another woman.

> KYNASTON *moves the fan to his left.*

KILLIGREW. And the left.

NED. Don't flirt with that woman.

KYNASTON *turns to* NELL *and makes a provocative gesture with the fan.*

Edward!

KILLIGREW. I think perhaps we'll ignore that one. Now, let's give Miss Gwynn a character. Dryden?

DRYDEN. Ooh – a bumptious country girl!

KILLIGREW. How original. (*To* NELL.) Perhaps you could conjure a few lines, or –

NELL. I could sing you a ditty?

KILLIGREW. Why not? When you're ready.

NELL *begins to mimic the fan gestures which she's learnt from* KYNASTON. *She turns it on. Her fan flirtation is brilliant. The men are all entranced... except* KYNASTON, *who is horrified.*

NELL (*singing*).
Here dwells a pretty maid whose name is Sis,
If you've a mind you may come in and kiss –
Her hole, her hole, her holey, holey hole –

KYNASTON. Stop, STOP!

NELL (*continuing her song*).
Her whole Estate is sev'nteen pence a year.
Yet you may kiss her if you come but near.

NELL, *now enjoying herself, continues, with the musicians now in full swing.*

Sis meets a farmer taller than an oak,
Lays down his fork and calls on her to stroke –
His cock, his cock, his cocky, cocky cock,
His cocker spaniel yelping at his knee
Oh shan't you stroke him, Sis? Oh Sis, for me!

Sis and the farmer they decide to wed,
Sun going down and when they go to bed
They bang, they bang, they bangy, bangy –

KYNASTON (*interrupting*). Enough! No woman can play a woman as well as I can play a woman!

KILLIGREW. We must follow the fashion.

KYNASTON. Fashions die. Trust me. An actor-ess? It'll never last. And I shall not be party to it – (*Going.*)

KILLIGREW. Edward!

KYNASTON. I'd rather chew the toenail off a dead leper! (*Exits.*)

DRYDEN. But my play!

NANCY. Hey! Not out there with your show shoes on! (*Chasing* KYNASTON *off.*)

DRYDEN. Come back! (*Following* KYNASTON *off.*)

KILLIGREW. Oh sot. Hell, what have we got to lose? (*To* NELL.) You'll start on two shillings a week. (*Gives her a pouch of coins.*) But watch your manners. We don't need any more drama.

NELL. Not at the playhouse.

KILLIGREW. And none of your cheek.

NELL. Sir.

KILLIGREW (*handing her a role*). Here. Read Florimel. Have it learnt by the end of the week. Now, if you will excuse me, I seem to have a raging fire to put out. Kynaston! (*Exits.*)

HART. I told you not to provoke him.

NELL (*flirting*). Didn't you like my song? (*Singing.*) 'Here dwells a pretty maid…'

She beckons him with her fan.

HART. 'Come here.' All right then.

He moves towards her. She runs her fingers through the fan's spokes.

'You want to talk to me.'

She puts the fan in front of her face and peers over the top.

'We are being watched'? (*Looks around.*) We're not.

NELL *indicates that* NED *is watching.*

Ned!

NED. Sorry.

NED *scuttles off. She fans herself quickly.*

HART. 'You don't care about me in the least'?

NELL. Damn. No. Wait.

She places the fan on her hand.

HART. 'Kiss you on the hand.'

He does. She moves the fan to her cheek.

'Kiss you... on the cheek.'

He does. She moves the fan to her mouth.

'Kiss you... kiss you...' (*Suddenly aware that they might be caught.*) What, here?

NELL. It's all right. No one's watching.

HART *turns and looks directly at the audience. Awkward. Then cuts his losses. Big snog.*

Scene Four

Medea

A room in the Palace. There is an easel on stage. Huge fanfare with pomp, ceremony and golden regalia. Liveried SERVANTS *stand at the ready as the trumpets herald the arrival of His Majesty* KING CHARLES II. CHARLES *bursts in in full monarchical get-up. Everyone bows as he strides into the centre of the room and proclaims –*

CHARLES. Where's Barbara?!

ARLINGTON. Your Majesty?

CHARLES. I thought she was having her portrait painted.

ARLINGTON. She was.

CHARLES. Well?

ARLINGTON. I'm afraid she and Mr Lely didn't quite see eye to eye.

CHARLES. Oh?

ARLINGTON. She asked to be painted as Venus.

CHARLES. But Lucy Walter is Venus.

ARLINGTON. Precisely.

CHARLES. So who… who *did* he paint her as?

ARLINGTON. Medea.

CHARLES. Hell and furies.

ARLINGTON. And now he's with the Royal Physician, having a paintbrush removed from his nostril.

CHARLES. Why do women have to complicate everything? (*Going*.) Where is she?

ARLINGTON. Sir – please! Parliament needs an answer on the hearth tax.

CHARLES. Not now.

ARLINGTON. But the Ministers –

CHARLES. The Ministers can wait. I cannot concentrate!

ARLINGTON. Might I assist?

CHARLES. Arlington, don't be a clodpoll. You know I can't think when I haven't… been satisfied. Now where on earth is –

SERVANT (*announcing*). Barbara Castlemaine, Your Majesty.

LADY CASTLEMAINE *arrives*.

LADY CASTLEMAINE. You should have that dunce sent to the gallows. Your infant son could have painted a better likeness.

CHARLES. Even so, I do wish you wouldn't injure my courtiers.

LADY CASTLEMAINE. Medea!

CHARLES. At least she's feisty. And I do like a woman with spunk.

LADY CASTLEMAINE and CHARLES look at each other. Chemistry oozes. She looks at the rest of the assembled COURT.

LADY CASTLEMAINE (*quietly*). Get out.

They leave. ARLINGTON *stays.*

All of you.

ARLINGTON. Ma'am. (*Exits.*)

CHARLES *and* LADY CASTLEMAINE *are left alone.*

CHARLES. Where have you been? I missed you.

LADY CASTLEMAINE. He embarrassed me, Charles. I won't have it.

CHARLES. He shan't do it again.

LADY CASTLEMAINE. No, I made sure of that. He shan't be able to sit for a week.

CHARLES. Sit? I thought the brush went up his nostril?

LADY CASTLEMAINE. Darling, he's an artist. He has a whole collection of brushes.

CHARLES. *Had* a whole collection. I shouldn't think he'll use them again.

LADY CASTLEMAINE. Not unless he's really trying to revolutionise the art world.

CHARLES. You do have a filthy mind. Come here.

They embrace. She pulls away.

LADY CASTLEMAINE. Tell me what you want.

CHARLES. Isn't it obvious?

LADY CASTLEMAINE. Tell me.

CHARLES. I want you, Barbara. Your mouth, your –

She lets him embrace her for a second then stops him.

LADY CASTLEMAINE. Wait – What about what I want?

CHARLES. What *you* want? (*Taken aback.*) Oh. Well? What do you want?

LADY CASTLEMAINE. Kiss my neck. Slowly.

He does.

Now kiss me here – (*Indicates her collarbone.*) gently. (*As he's kissing her.*) Put Clarendon to death.

CHARLES (*pulling away*). What?! But he's my Chief Minister!

LADY CASTLEMAINE. He is in your way.

CHARLES. He's your cousin! Have you no loyalty?

LADY CASTLEMAINE. We're losing our grip on the Channel. He will sink us, Charles. Rebuild the fleet –

CHARLES. We don't have the funds.

LADY CASTLEMAINE. Because he has squandered them! Give Arlington the Treasury, and we'll be the greatest traders in Europe.

CHARLES. It wouldn't be good for relations.

LADY CASTLEMAINE. What sort of monarch do you want to be? A flaccid, feeble, slapsack of a man? Or a mighty king with a sceptre hard as rock.

CHARLES. I love it when you talk defence strategy.

CHARLES *goes to kiss her. She moves off.*

LADY CASTLEMAINE. Not so fast. I'll meet you in your chamber.

CHARLES. What's wrong with here? Now?!

LADY CASTLEMAINE. No. Wait. I've had an outfit shipped from India. Inspired by a little Sanskrit book with the most extraordinary illustrations. I'll follow you directly.

CHARLES. Be quick! Before I explode like a Spanish warship.

CHARLES *goes, in a state of excitement.* ARLINGTON *emerges from his hideaway.*

ARLINGTON. Barbara!

LADY CASTLEMAINE. You got what you wanted, didn't you? Clarendon's as good as dead. And once he's gone, the Dutch won't stand a chance.

ARLINGTON. He won't attack the Dutch, he cares too much for William.

LADY CASTLEMAINE. Leave William to me.

ARLINGTON. You wouldn't?! He's only a boy.

LADY CASTLEMAINE. Precisely. He is ripe for the plucking. And as the Dutch descend into hell, you, my dear, can revel in your ascendance.

ARLINGTON. And you in yours, 'my lady'.

LADY CASTLEMAINE. It'll do for now.

ARLINGTON. For now?! Barbara, don't push him.

LADY CASTLEMAINE. Arlington, I am the King's beloved. His paramour. His muse. And I am rewarded generously for my services to King and country.

ARLINGTON. If only the King knew how much of the country you were servicing.

LADY CASTLEMAINE. I could have you sent to Tyburn, your tongue cut out and your entrails knitted into a pisspot for my dead dog to take a shit in.

ARLINGTON. We need each other. If you lose his favour, we both lose his ear.

LADY CASTLEMAINE. I have more than his ear, my friend. Now, if you please, the King awaits.

ARLINGTON. Go on, lie back and think of England.

LADY CASTLEMAINE. Lie back? Oh, Arlington. No wonder you never got further in politics.

She leaves. He watches her go, uneasy.

Scene Five

The Mask of Florimel

KYNASTON, DRYDEN, NED *and* KILLIGREW *arrive for the rehearsal.*

KYNASTON. She's not here. She's not here! I knew it! I'll get into costume.

DRYDEN. She is here.

KYNASTON. Are you sure?

NED. She's in the dressing room.

KYNASTON. Poxing hell.

KILLIGREW. Why don't we look at the final act while we're waiting. Dryden?

DRYDEN. Ah yes. About that.

KILLIGREW. Dryden?

DRYDEN. It's almost done.

KILLIGREW. Let me see.

NED. Have you written a line for me?

DRYDEN (*handing* KILLIGREW *a scrumpled scroll with multiple crossings out*). Sir.

KILLIGREW. Where's the rest of it?

DRYDEN. It's nearly there, the prologue's done now, and the middle bit, it's just the ending.

KILLIGREW. Well, the ending's pretty vital, isn't it – dramatically? We're not going for a groundbreaking new form of theatre where there's a beginning, a middle and a very long pause! For goodness' sake – we open next week! We don't have an audience, we don't have an ending and we seem to be missing a leading lady.

KYNASTON. I'll do it!

KILLIGREW. Absolutely not! Nell is to play Florimel and you are to play Flavia (*Pronounced with a long 'a' as in 'bra'.*) as we agreed.

KYNASTON. As you insisted.

> HART *arrives with* NELL, NANCY *and* ROSE. NELL *is wearing a splendid dress.*

NANCY. Told you she'd scrub up all right.

NED. Fig me.

KILLIGREW. You do look very... female.

KYNASTON (*looking at* ROSE). And who's this?

NELL. My sister.

KYNASTON (*to* KILLIGREW). Are we to have the whole scurvy pack of them descend on us?

NELL. Well, my dad's dead and my mother's a drunk so probably not.

KILLIGREW. Rehearsals are supposed to be private –

NELL. She just wants to watch.

ROSE. I can help.

NANCY. Can you sew?

ROSE. Course.

NANCY. How's your sense of smell?

> NANCY *indicates a basket of dirty stockings for darning. They sit down and start sewing.*

KILLIGREW. Well. I... fine. Let's start with Scene Three – and hope that Miss Gwynn remembers her lines.

HART. Well, if Dryden didn't insist on changing them –

DRYDEN. I'm just trying to get it right!

KILLIGREW. Well, maybe next time you could get it right before we start rehearsals. Now, we begin in the park, by moonlight. Florimel and Celadon are wildly in love – but rumour has it he's been amorous with other women.

NELL (*to* HART, *warmly*). The devil!

KILLIGREW. So she sets him a trap. Nancy, the mask if you will.

NANCY hands NELL a mask on a stick.

ROSE. Oh, I like that.

KYNASTON. Oh, please.

KILLIGREW. And onwards, Mr Hart.

Perhaps musicians begin to play.

HART. 'What angel do I see here? (*Blocking her path.*) I' faith, Lady Bright, I am got betwixt you and home. You are my prisoner until you resolve me one question.'

She makes a melodramatic sign that she is dumb.

'Pox, I think she's dumb!'

NELL *makes a coy gesture.*

'Indeed? Then thou canst tell no tales.'

He goes to kiss her. She holds her fan up to stop him.

NELL. 'Hold, hold!'

HART. 'Ah! You have found your tongue!'

NELL. ''Twas time, I think. What had become of me… (*Drying.*) What had become of me…'

KILLIGREW. 'If I had not'!

NELL. 'If I had not.'

KILLIGREW. Come on!

HART. 'You are infinitely handsome. They may talk of Florimel, but in faith she must come short of you.'

NELL. 'Have you seen this Florimel?'

HART. 'I looked a little that way, but I had soon enough of her.'

NELL. 'Indeed? They say you are betrothed.'

KYNASTON *enters as Flavia.*

KYNASTON. 'Florimel, you are called within.'

A beat. Everyone looks at KYNASTON, who is supposed to have exited.

HART. Edward?

KYNASTON. What?

HART. That's your cue to leave.

KILLIGREW. All right, let's go back – we'll go from / 'Indeed'.

KYNASTON. I don't think it's clear.

KILLIGREW. What?

KYNASTON. Flavia should tell us why Florimel must return inside.

KILLIGREW. She doesn't need to.

KYNASTON. Of course she does. The audience doesn't know why Florimel must go in. There must be a pressing reason.

HART. It's just a device.

KYNASTON. A device?

DRYDEN. I just put it in as a feed, Ed.

KYNASTON. A 'feed'?

KILLIGREW. So let's move / on.

KYNASTON. But it doesn't explain why Flavia asks.

HART. Oh, come / on.

KYNASTON. What is Flavia's reason? What is Flavia's impetus for posing the question?

NELL. Does it really matter?

KYNASTON. It matters to Flavia!

DRYDEN. But it doesn't affect the scene.

KYNASTON. Of course it does! Mr Dryden, if you could just write me a short monologue to / reveal –

KILLIGREW. Ed, it's not really Flavia's scene.

KYNASTON. I'm quite aware of that, thank you.

HART. And we open in a week.

KYNASTON. I'm not coming on for two lines. It's mortifying.

NELL. One line.

KYNASTON. What?

NELL. One line. You put a pause in, but there isn't one. So really you should do it on one breath. (*Beat.*) It's one line.

Beat.

KYNASTON. You'll have to find someone else.

DRYDEN. But my play!

KYNASTON. Oh, don't you worry, Mr Dryden. Actresses are two a penny. Just ask the next cheap whore who offers you a citrus fruit! (*Exits.*)

KILLIGREW. Ed? Ed! (*To* HART.) You said you'd schooled her. (*Taking* NED *in.*) And that you'd practised!

NED. It's not her fault; it takes so much longer when you can't read!

NELL. Ned!

HART. Ned!

KILLIGREW. She can't read?!!

HART *points at the exit.* NED *goes.*

NELL. Sir, I'll practise!

KILLIGREW. I don't believe this. Edward! (*Exits, following* KILLIGREW.)

HART. Let me talk to him. (*Exits.*)

NELL. Sorry.

DRYDEN. It's not your fault. It's my writing – it's desperate. I think I'll scrap it and start again. Again.

NELL. But it's good.

DRYDEN. It's not. Is it?

NELL. I like the way you write.

DRYDEN. Do you? You know, sometimes I just can't get the dratted thing from quill to parchment. I have an idea but it just goes pfff! It wouldn't be quite so torturous if Johnny wasn't so 'inspired' all the time.

NELL. Johnny?

DRYDEN. My cousin. Everyone's always 'Jonathan this, Jonathan that – isn't Jonathan dazzling.'

NELL. He's a playwright?

DRYDEN. He wants to be. Though his work's quite unstageable. He's got this idea about a shipwrecked man who gets marooned in a land full of tiny people. How do you put that on stage?

NELL. He should write it as a book instead.

DRYDEN. Good idea! Get him off my tail.

NELL. Why do you fret about what folk think anyway? You don't get nervous, do you?

DRYDEN. No. (*Beat.*) Yes. Yes I do actually. I get this ringing in my ears, it's damnable. I'm not like you.

NELL. I haven't been on yet.

DRYDEN. But you're not afraid. And you have a way, when we're watching you.

ROSE. She's always had that.

DRYDEN. I, on the other hand, have to wrench this out like a rotten tooth, a pussing carbuncle, yeurch.

He holds the scrumpled piece of paper at arm's length.

NELL. What's wrong with it?

DRYDEN. It's predictable! Boy meets girl, girl resists, boy persuades her. Kiss. Marriage. Happy ending.

NANCY. Read it to us.

ROSE. Go on.

DRYDEN. Alright. So – it is night. The air is chilly, stars pepper the sky and, in the park, the masked lady reveals herself as Florimel. (*Playing Celadon, surprised.*) 'Florimel?!' (*In a lady's voice, as Florimel.*) 'At your service. The same kind and coming Florimel you have described.' (*As Celadon.*) 'Florimel?! Ha! I knew at once that we were good for nothing but each other. Let us be married at once!' (*As Florimel.*) 'Married at once?' (*As Celadon.*) 'By Jove, yes. And do you consent?' (*As Florimel.*) 'Yes!' Then they embrace and... (*From* NELL*'s expression.*) What?

NELL. She says yes? To that?!

DRYDEN. What's wrong with it?

Pause. The girls erupt into laughter.

NELL. There's no 'boom!'

DRYDEN. Boom?

NELL. Spark. Gunpowder.

DRYDEN. What are you saying? It lacks fire?

NELL. Yep.

DRYDEN. Not even a flicker? A tiny glow? An ember?

NELL. Nope.

DRYDEN *looks to* NANCY *and* ROSE.

NANCY. Nope.

ROSE. Sorry.

DRYDEN. I knew it, it's just kindling!

NELL. Don't sulk.

DRYDEN. It's just a romance, no one listens anyway –

NELL. So make 'em listen. Grab 'em by the scallies.

DRYDEN. Sorry?

NANCY. And stop apologising.

DRYDEN. Sorry.

NELL. Mr Dryden! Yet again, some gallant falls for a wilting, waifish woman without a bean of personality or a single funny line, but hey, it doesn't matter, cos she's pretty –

DRYDEN. Now wait a minute –

NELL. And what does this flimsy whimsy want from life? Adventure? Respect? No... all she wants is this flopsome fop cos once he wrote her a poem and compared her to a flower. Is that what you think women want?

DRYDEN. Well, I –

GIRLS. No!

NELL. Mr Dryden! It's not! We're as knotty and tangly as you are, and yet how do you write us? 'Oh Romeo, Romeo, lend me your dagger so I can kill myself – for though I'm young and healthy and have everything to live for – and I only met you a week ago – my life's not worth living now you've gone.' Really? It's hogswill. Juliet is a noodle. Who wrote that twaddle anyway?

DRYDEN. William Shakespeare.

NELL. Well, he should learn to write proper plays. Or let his wife have a go. Please, Mr Dryden. You can write for a real woman now. No one has done that before. Write from here – (*Indicating her guts.*) and write me a character! With skin and heart and some sense in her head. Celadon says he thinks he *might* marry her. You think she'd agree – to *that*?!

DRYDEN. Wouldn't she?

GIRLS. No!

DRYDEN. What would she say?

NANCY. You're the writer!

DRYDEN. She bids him... she bids him – 'Wait!'

NELL (*in character*). 'Wait!'

DRYDEN. 'These shallow protestations of love – they're not sufficient!'

NELL (*in character*). 'Not sufficient!'

DRYDEN. She's no vacuous tart –

NANCY. Bit far.

DRYDEN. She challenges him! If he's to win her, he must prove himself. She wants a lover who'd – who'd what?

NELL. Hang himself!

NANCY. Drown himself!

ROSE. Break his neck!

DRYDEN. Poison himself for very despair! He that will scruple that is an impudent fellow if he says he is in love.

NELL. Though he's only a man – he cannot hang, drown, break his neck *and* poison himself at the same time.

DRYDEN. That's funny – that's good!

NELL. That is Celadon's comeback. He must be a wit too, or she'd never look twice at him.

DRYDEN. Is that so? (*Now frantically scribbling.*) This is gold – it's gold!

NELL. Then she sets him a challenge.

DRYDEN. Yes! (*Pause.*) What challenge?

NELL. Now that is where the master playwright comes into his own.

DRYDEN. I've got it.

NELL. Gunpowder?

DRYDEN. Guy Fawkes, my dear.

GIRLS. Boom!

DRYDEN. Boom!

HART (*arriving*). Boom?

DRYDEN. Mr Hart, you have found us a marvel.

HART. She's a marvel with lines to learn.

NELL. I've learnt most of them.

HART. That was only Act One, Nell. Of five. (*Holding up four giant roles*.) We've got one week.

NELL *looks at* HART *in horror. One week?! Yikes.*

Song – 'One Week to Go'

During which the COMPANY *prepares for the play: a montage of rehearsals, training, dance lessons, getting into costume, etc.*

ALL (*singing*). Hark the bonny bell,
　　　Hear the merry knell,
　　　Know that all is well,
　　　One week to go!

　　　Don the ruffs, the periwigs,
　　　Drain the pottles, suck the figs,
　　　Round the circle, merry jigs,
　　　One week to go!

　　　Skip the triplet, dance the dandle,
　　　Don the doublet, light the candle,
　　　Brace the basket by the handle,
　　　Six days to go!

　　　Cotton up my bodkin,
　　　Button up my jerkin,
　　　Plumping up my merkin,
　　　Five days to go!

　　　Hark the bonny bell,
　　　Hear the merry knell,
　　　Know that all is well,
　　　Four days to go!

　　　Pas de deux and minuet,
　　　Rouge a cheek, and trill duet,
　　　Stuff a codpiece for a bet,
　　　Three days to go!

　　　Lace the bootles, fill the bumpers,
　　　Sound the horns and beat the thumpers
　　　Darn the stockings, hem the humpers,
　　　Two days to go!

Now we don disguises,
Practise our devises,
As the curtain rises,
One day to go!

Scourge the pockmarks from the pate,
Cover up the poxéd state
'Tis the time for fun not fate,
One hour to go!

Time hot-footed now is sprung,
Hours, moments have we none,
For 'tis time we were begun.
One minute!

Into…

Scene Six

First-night Nerves

In the dressing room, NELL *is suffering from a fit of nerves when* ROSE *bursts in.*

ROSE. What are you doing back here?

NELL. I can't feel my legs.

ROSE. It's packed out front.

NELL. That's all I need to hear.

ROSE. Come / on.

NELL. I can't do it.

ROSE. You know it. You've practised.

NELL. My head's full of dust –

HART (*off*). Nell?!

NELL. I'm going home.

ROSE. Nell! They've never seen a woman up there before. You going to let some other wench take that from you? Hey! What would your dad say? If he could see you now?

HART *and* NANCY *burst in.*

NANCY. Found her!

HART. Are you all right?

NELL. I think I'm going to faint.

NANCY. Have a nose of this.

NANCY *sticks some smelling salts under* NELL*'s nose and it sends her reeling.*

NELL. Jesus Mary! Gimme some more.

KYNASTON, DRYDEN *and* KILLIGREW *enter.*

KILLIGREW. Ready?

NELL. No.

ROSE. Yes, she's ready.

KILLIGREW. Everyone feels a little querulous their first time.

KYNASTON. I didn't.

NELL. Charles, you're spinning…

HART. Nell. Look at me. Breathe. In. Out. And just think through the words of the song.

NELL. Song? What song?!

Music starts up.

DRYDEN. That song!

NED (*arriving at speed*). You're on, you're on!

NELL. I'm going to be sick.

KYNASTON. Aim it at the groundlings – they only paid a fiver.

A trumpet fanfare – the song begins with the CHORUS *singing.*

Song – 'Celadon and Florimel'

CHORUS (*singing*).
> Come, come, come
> Let us tell, tell, tell,
> Let us tell, tell, tell of Florimel
> And Celadon her true love.
> And Celadon her true love.
> Will lovers sigh and passion fly?
> Or must he find a new love?
>
> Two souls, entwined, our lovers are
> Whose poles align under fortune's star
> And here comes one –
> (*As* HART *enters*.) 'Tis Celadon!
> Whom all the maidens gaze upon.
> He hath many mistress conquered.
> He hath the ladies sighing.

HART (*singing*).
> There's but one maid I can't persuade!

CHORUS (*singing, aside*).
> And not for want of trying.
> Celadon loves Florimel.

HART (*singing*).
> There's only one maid for me.
> The fairest Florimel I love,
> Oh how she will adore me!

CHORUS (*singing*).
> Her damask cheeks, her ringlets sleek.

HART (*singing*).
> Her bounteous peaks.

CHORUS (*singing*).
> She's come!

NELL *enters as Florimel. On seeing the audience, she seizes up completely.*

HART (*singing*).
> Be silent, ye, for hark she speaks…

NELL *is frozen and doesn't sing. The musicians stop. Silence.* HART *cues her in.*

(*Whispered.*) 'Oh, how my heart doth cower.'

HART *cues the musicians to play again.* NELL *makes an attempt to sing the next verse, but she's too nervous.*

NELL (*singing fitfully*).
　　　Oh… how my heart doth cower,
　　　I was to see my lover here.
　　　He promised here to meet me…

The song grinds to a halt. Silence. NELL *starts to leave the stage, then stops with her back to us. A beat. She rallies and begins to sing. It's a song from her childhood, a song she knows well.*

　　　(*Singing.*) I can dance and I can sing,
　　　And I am good at either.
　　　And I can do the t'other thing
　　　When we get together.

Turning to the audience.

　　　I have lately lost my dear,
　　　'Twas a holy brother.
　　　If he do not meet me here,
　　　In faith I'll get another!

NELL *throws caution to the wind and dances. She is brilliant. The* MUSICIANS, *then the* COMPANY, *join in. The song builds…*

　　　I can nimbly come above,
　　　And I can tumble under,
　　　And I'll dance in wet and wind,
　　　And I'll sing at thunder,
　　　Said my love he'd meet me here,
　　　He would make me gladder,
　　　But if he do not appear
　　　In faith, t'won't make me sadder!

　　　A Dutchman loves his pipe and can,
　　　A Jew does love his Turk well,
　　　But I could love a country man

For he will do his work well.
But if he do not make me hay,
If he is a thumpkin,
I'll not give myself away
To any old country bumpkin!

I will shun the bumpkin, aye,
I will wait for better,
I will have a clever man,
Who can write a letter,
But if he don't love me well,
If there's no romancing,
I'll leave him alone to dwell,
And I will go on dancing!

It's a triumph. A star is born.

Scene Seven

Hart's Strumpet

Cut to HART *and* NELL *outside the theatre after the performance – she's just found him.*

NELL. Charlie? They've opened a barrel inside. What are you doing? Oh Lord – you didn't like it.

HART. Nell.

NELL. I know I missed a cue – and buggered the jig – and cut off Mr Kynaston – but it's a lot to remember –

HART. Nell.

NELL. And I'll get it right tomorrow – I promise – I just – (*Pause*.) What?

HART. You really don't know, do you?

NELL. Know what?

HART. Good God.

NELL. What?

HART. It was extraordinary.

NELL. What was?

HART. Didn't you hear them, Nell? They loved you.

NELL. They loved us.

HART. They've never seen anything like it. You were luminous. And you were real. A real woman. I'm not sure we'll ever go back. It changes everything.

Beat.

NELL. Come with me.

HART. Where are we going?

NELL. Up.

HART. Up where?

NELL. On the roof!

HART (*alarmed*). Why?! Why would we do that?

NELL. I've something to show you.

HART. What?

NELL. London.

HART. Can't we see it from here? On the nice sturdy, solid ground?

NELL. Don't be feeble.

HART. Heights make me giddy.

NELL. You're not a coward.

HART. I might be.

NELL. You're not. I've seen you address a thousand men.

HART. Yes but –

NELL. And tonight.

HART. Tonight what?

NELL. Tonight you risked your name on a 'strumpet'.

Pause.

HART. So I did. My strumpet.

They might kiss. She breaks away and heads up the ladder.
HART *doesn't move.*

NELL (*singing, quietly*). '*I can sing and I can dance…*' Come on… I'm still wearing my Florimel stockings.

HART. You're not.

She shows him a little peep then continues up the ladder.

Every time.

He follows her up.

Scene Eight

The Mistresses at War

QUEEN CATHERINE *of Braganza,* CHARLES*'s barren wife, arrives on stage in a fury. She is smashing everything in her sight.* ARLINGTON *and an array of* SERVANTS *are struggling to stop her. She talks in very fast, impassioned Portuguese.*

QUEEN. *Não posso acreditar nisso! Nenhuma inglesa seria tratada assim! Como ousa? Comedor de pudim, suino pálido!* [I cannot believe this. No English woman would be treated like this. How dare he! The eater of pudding, the pale-faced swine!]

ARLINGTON. *A Senhora?*

QUEEN. *Sai do meu caminho, pinto flácido. Tivesse eu nunca pisado no vosso país congelado estúpido. Vocês são todos bastardos!* [Get out of my way, you flaccid dick. I wish I'd never set foot in your stupid, frozen country. You're all bastards!]

She picks up a bust of CHARLES.

ARLINGTON. My lady, please – it's a Bernini – it's terribly –

She hurls the bust at the wall. It smashes.

Expensive.

CHARLES *arrives, obviously alerted to the crisis.*

CHARLES. What in heaven's name? (*Seeing the bust.*) Oh. My head.

ARLINGTON. Sir.

CHARLES. It was a Bernini; terribly expensive.

ARLINGTON. I think the Queen is suffering from an affliction of ill humour.

The QUEEN *spits on the floor in his direction.*

CHARLES. She's not angry with me, is she?

ARLINGTON. Allow me to enquire.

CHARLES (*under his breath*). I think per/haps you shouldn't.

ARLINGTON (*to the* QUEEN). *O Rei gostaria de saber, a senhora, se você está irritado com ele.* [The King would like to know, Madam, if you are angry with him.]

QUEEN. *Irritado? Eu, irritado? Irritaola? Pareço irritado? Estou tão furiosa que peço meu Deus para golpear-lo, e queimar suas entranhas; para enviar-lo ao inferno onde o diabo pode banquetear-se com os restos carbonizados. Sim, estou irritada, estou furiosa!* [Angry? Me, angry? Do I seem angry? I am so angry I ask my God to smite him down, to burn his entrails to coals and to send him to hell where the devil can feast on his charred remains. Yes I am angry, I am in a fury!]

ARLINGTON. She says… yes. I shall enquire further.

CHARLES. I / wouldn't.

QUEEN. *Estou chateada porque O Rei fedorento nomeou sua puta, a primeira dama da minha câmara real! Acch, essa prostituta, Barbara Castlemaine!* [I am upset because the stinking King named his whore the First Lady of my royal bedchamber. Ugh! That prostitute, Barbara Castlemaine!]

ARLINGTON. Barbara Castlemaine?

CHARLES. Oh / no.

QUEEN. *Sim!* [Yes!]

ARLINGTON. *Nao!* [No!]

QUEEN. *Sim!* [Yes!]

ARLINGTON. Sir! What on earth possessed you?

CHARLES. I thought perhaps –

ARLINGTON. Perhaps what? They'd enjoy an exchange of girlish pleasantries before bed?

CHARLES. I thought the Queen might be lonely.

ARLINGTON. You cannot make your mistress First Lady of the Queen's bedchamber! Good God, sir! Of all the women in the Court, in the country – there's no one the Queen hates more than –

SERVANT. Lady Castlemaine, Your Majesty.

LADY CASTLEMAINE *strolls in, looking pleased with herself.*

LADY CASTLEMAINE. You called?

QUEEN. *Ela!* [Her!]

CHARLES. Oh no.

QUEEN. *Sua puta! Vagabunda! Demônio insensivel!* [Slut! Vagabond! Callous she-devil!]

LADY CASTLEMAINE. The Queen seems a little perturbed. Is it the Spanish flu?

QUEEN. *Sou portuguesa, sua imbecil! Tirat essa prostituta pestilenta da minha vista!* [I'm Portuguese, you imbecile. Get that pestilent whore out of my sight!] (*In broken English.*) O, senhor, sir, I am your Queen, your wife. I honour you for the good of my country. But this, you insult me. You hurt me in my heart.

She leaves in silence.

CHARLES (*to* LADY CASTLEMAINE). Why can't you just –
be friends?

LADY CASTLEMAINE. Don't blame me if your lunatic wife
is racked by paroxysms. She is a slave to the vapours. No
wonder she is barren.

CHARLES. Madam, you go too far. Do not forget that your
place here is according to my will.

LADY CASTLEMAINE *stops. She turns to the* SERVANTS.

LADY CASTLEMAINE. Get out.

They leave. She turns to CHARLES.

How can you insult me in front of them? They will not
respect me.

CHARLES. Then earn their respect. And mine.

LADY CASTLEMAINE. Sir!

CHARLES. You ask too much – you both do. You make my
head ache. I'm going to the theatre.

ARLINGTON. Sir, you know Parliament's aversion to
theatricals. I really don't know what you see in it.

CHARLES. Joy, Arlington! That's what. Joy – and gaiety – and
a complete absence of complicated women.

CHARLES *leaves. The others follow.*

Scene Nine

A Very Important Guest

Cut to mid-scene on stage. HART and NELL are magnificent. They're like Beatrice and Benedick, both playing a good deal to the audience.

NELL. 'Have you seen this Florimel?'

HART. 'I looked a little that way, but I had soon enough of her.'

NELL. 'Indeed? They say you are betrothed.'

KYNASTON *enters as Flavia and looks around for* NELL.

KYNASTON. 'Florimel, you are called within.'

HART. 'Florimel?!'

KYNASTON *stands, reluctant to leave, looking over the audience. Finally he makes his exit.*

NELL. 'At your service. The same kind and coming Florimel that you have described.'

HART. 'Then you have counterfeit to deceive me?! I knew at once that we were good for nothing but each other. Florimel, let us be married at once!'

NELL. 'Married at once?'

HART. 'By Jove, yes. And do you, oh beauteous Florimel, consent?'

HART *goes to embrace her – she stops him, enjoying* DRYDEN*'s rewrite.*

NELL. 'No. I shall not marry you yet. For I must have proof of love before I can believe it. I would have a lover that would hang himself, drown himself, break his neck, poison himself for very despair. He that will scruple that is an impudent fellow if he says he is in love.'

CHARLES *arrives in the Royal Box. Everyone turns to look at* CHARLES – HART *bows to him;* NELL *hasn't seen him and continues, oblivious.*

HART (*hushed*). Nell!

NELL. What? (*Seeing him.*) Oh!

> NELL *meets his eyes. She curtsies.*

CHARLES. Don't let me interrupt. Play on!

HART. 'Pray, madam, which of the four things would you have me do? For a man's but a man. He cannot hang, drown, break his neck, and poison himself all together.'

> NELL *begins to play, just a little, to* CHARLES.

NELL. 'Well then, because you were but a beginner, any of these should do.'

> HART, *trying to hide his frustration, attempts to place himself between* NELL *and* CHARLES.

HART. 'I am much deceived in those eyes of yours if a treat, a song and the fiddles be not more acceptable proof of love than any of those tragical ones you have mentioned.'

NELL. 'Oh, but you must be pale and melancholic to show that you are in love. And that I shall require of you when I see you next.'

> HART *is getting increasingly jealous.*

HART. 'When shall I see you next?'

NELL. 'Shall I make a proposition to you? I will give you a whole year of probation to love me in. To grow reserved, discreet, sober and faithful, and to pay me all the services of a lover.'

HART. 'And at the end, will you marry me?'

NELL (*turning to* CHARLES). What do you think, Your Majesty?

CHARLES. I think you should wait for a better offer.

> NELL *smiles at* CHARLES, *who is entranced. She takes a deep curtsey, and then one separately to* CHARLES. HART, *meanwhile, is dying inside.*

Scene Ten

The Finest English Sausage

Minutes later, NELL *returns to the dressing room. She's in a spin.* NANCY *and* ROSE *are there to help her change.* HART *storms in. He pays no heed to the other two girls.*

ROSE. The King, Nelly!

NANCY. The blooming King!

HART. What were you thinking?

NELL. What?

HART. The love scene. You played it all to him.

NELL. I did not.

HART. I was there, Nell. Waiting for a single, solitary glance.

NELL. I looked at you.

HART. Hardly.

NELL. I was playing to the punters. You taught me that.

HART. And I regret it.

NELL. Charlie –

HART. I couldn't concentrate! I can't perform if I'm thinking of someone else.

NANCY. That's a man's trouble. Women do it all the time.

HART. You humiliated me. In front of them! The way he looked at you –

NELL. I'm on the stage. He was only looking.

HART. Don't you see? If he wants you, he has you. So for God's sake, don't tempt him. All right? (*Beat.*) All right?

CHARLES *arrives in the doorway.*

CHARLES. Knock, knock.

HART (*without turning round*). Come back later.

CHARLES. Busy later.

HART. Can't you see we're… (*Turning round, seeing* CHARLES.) Oh God.

CHARLES. Well – King. Next rung down. Look, would you mind…

He indicates that he wants to be left alone with NELL. HART *doesn't want to leave*.

HART. Sir, we're about to go back on.

CHARLES. Just – do a jig, will you? Or a tinkly bit on the lute. Keep them entertained. (*Pause*.) Off you go.

They all make to go, including NELL.

Not you, Gwynn.

NELL. Your Majesty.

A beat. HART *exits, fuming, followed by* NANCY *and* ROSE. NELL *and* CHARLES *look at each other*.

CHARLES. Weren't you getting changed? Don't let me stop you.

NELL. It's thruppence for the peeping fee.

CHARLES. I thought it was a penny.

NELL. Shouldn't you be watching the play?

CHARLES. I was bored. The main attraction's gone.

NELL. What's that then?

CHARLES. The finest actor in the King's Company.

NELL. Nothing like being in the King's company.

CHARLES. You seem to have made quite a stir. You think it's an improvement, having women on my stage?

NELL. Course. 'Specially a woman from Cheapside.

CHARLES. Cheapside?

NELL. Oh, it's a marvellous place, besides the corpses and the stink of slop. Maybe you should call by.

CHARLES. Maybe I will. Really, nobles are so tedious, between talking to a dead body and the Duke of Cambridge I'd take the corpse every time.

NELL. It can't be all bad, being King. Do you like it?

CHARLES. Like… being King?

NELL. Yep. Why? You never been asked before?

CHARLES. Never. Folk are usually too busy grovelling at my feet. Not you though.

NELL. Not me, no.

CHARLES. Dine with me tonight.

NELL. Sir?!

CHARLES. After the play.

NELL. You said you were busy later.

CHARLES. I am. I'm taking you for supper.

Beat.

NELL. I have plans.

CHARLES. What plans?!

NELL. I'm learning lines with Mr Hart.

CHARLES. Ah, he's the lover, is he?

NELL. He's Celadon, yes.

Beat.

CHARLES. And afterwards?

NELL. It's Thursday. I'm having a bath.

CHARLES. You smell divine. Don't wash.

NELL. Oh, I must, sir. Underneath here I'm filthy.

CHARLES. I'll bet you are. But a girl must eat – let me tempt you. Roast hog. Very wild boar. The finest English sausage.

NELL. I couldn't. I only dine with gentlemen.

CHARLES. I am a gentleman!

NELL. Hardly, asking a girl for supper before you've even introduced yourself.

CHARLES. I'm Charles.

NELL. Charles who?

CHARLES. Charles Stuart!

NELL. Well, Charles Stuart. I am Nell Gwynn. (*Pause*.) You got a bath at your place?

CHARLES. Forty-three.

NELL. Oh.

CHARLES. What do you want, Nell Gwynn? Money?

NELL. No. I want you to answer my question. Do you like it? Being King.

CHARLES. Well... I don't want for anything. I can summon our finest soprano, I sup from the very best china.

NELL. But...?

CHARLES. I didn't say 'but'.

NELL. I saw it. In your face. You looked away. And your breath changed. You took a short breath.

CHARLES. Meaning what, exactly?

NELL. Meaning you're covering. You've got more in your pate than you're saying.

CHARLES. And what makes you so sure?

NELL. I'm an actress, sir. We trade in the language of the face. Go on. You sup from the very best china – but...

Pause.

CHARLES. But... my father was killed in front of a crowd. And I was there. I watched.

NELL. Sorry.

Pause.

CHARLES. People have expectations. Notions of what they want me to be.

NELL. I know all about that.

CHARLES. I suppose you do.

NELL. Still, I wouldn't swap.

CHARLES. Sorry?

NELL. Not being able to go where my feet take me or say what I like? I wouldn't be King for all your crown jewels.

CHARLES. That sounds like treason, young lady. I could have you strung up.

NELL. Now that would be a shame. If you had me killed in Act One, how'd you know what happens next?

CHARLES. Isn't it obvious? Boy meets girl, girl resists, then, after a bit of badinage... he bags her.

NELL. That's your experience, is it?

CHARLES. Every time.

NELL. You haven't been watching the right plays, sir. The girl in this tale isn't half so predictable.

Music.

And that's my cue. Anon. (*Exits.*)

CHARLES. I... (*Pause.*) Well, I'll be damned.

Scene Eleven

The Enchanted Island

The COMPANY *are all gathered in a crisis talk.*

DRYDEN. So, far away on a distant shore, there is a wizard, who lives on an island. And his name is Prospero!

NANCY. Wait a minute –

DRYDEN. With his daughter Miranda –

HART. Dryden, is this your / idea?

DRYDEN. And his other daughter, Dorinda.

NED/NANCY. / Oh!

KYNASTON. Oh! Dorinda?

DRYDEN. Then, when a ship is wrecked off the coast in a tempest… – (*Looking warily at the others.*) tempest… uous storm, some men are washed ashore!

NELL. Sounds exciting.

NANCY. Sounds familiar.

KILLIGREW. Enough of that. This is *The Enchanted Island* by Mr Dryden. It is an opera.

DRYDEN. No it's not.

KILLIGREW. Well, it's got songs in it. And dancing. And flying fish. Nell, you're to play Miranda; Kynaston, you're Dorinda…

KYNASTON. Is she a fine part?

DRYDEN. Indispensible.

NED. Who am I to play?

KILLIGREW. The mermaid. And Hart, you can cheer up. You're to play Prospero.

HART. The strapping young hero?

KILLIGREW. Well… I'm not sure 'strapping' is quite the word. Or 'young'. Or perhaps 'hero'. But it's a splendid part.

HART. He's the lover though?

KILLIGREW. Well, he loves… (*Searching*.) magic. And islands!

HART. He's not the lover?

KILLIGREW. Dryden?

DRYDEN. Well. Yes. Sort of. (*Pause*.) No. No, he's not.

HART. Why aren't I the lover?

KILLIGREW. Just a request. From above.

HART. From the Palace?!

KILLIGREW. Prospero's a bigger role, look!

KILLIGREW *shows* HART *the two roles; Prospero's is much bigger.*

HART. But I'm always the lover!

KILLIGREW. No time for debate. We don't have long. We open on Saturday.

ALL. Saturday! / What?! (*Etc*.)

KILLIGREW. I know it's a swift turnaround –

HART. We haven't even read it yet!

KILLIGREW. But His Majesty insists.

KYNASTON. Can't you put him off? He's been in every night.

KILLIGREW. And he wants to keep on coming.

DRYDEN. He loves it! He adores it! The King loves me! Maybe he'll make me a knight, or a baron. Baron von Dryden!

NANCY. Why would you be Baron von Dryden? You'd just be Baron Dryden.

DRYDEN. I'd be a baron, I could do what I like.

KILLIGREW. I think, in truth, the King is rather taken with our Florimel.

Everyone turns to look at NELL.

NELL. I didn't ask for it.

HART. And if he wants to come every night? What then? A play a day until he finds a new doxy for his fancy.

NELL. Charles.

HART (*reading the stage directions*). It says here Prospero is a wizened old man! I am the lover. I've always been the lover. I don't want to be some crusty old jester in a false beard – (*Unravelling the scroll and reading on incredulously.*) and a pointy hat!

KILLIGREW. That's just the stage directions. We can ignore them.

DRYDEN. No you can't!

KYNASTON. Charles, darling, remember this outrage and channel it into your performance, temples raised, nostrils flared –

HART. Shut up, Edward!

KYNASTON. Magnificent!

As KILLIGREW *speaks,* CHARLES *arrives – everyone else in the* COMPANY *notices.* KILLIGREW *continues without noticing.*

KILLIGREW. Listen. However you're feeling, just cast it aside. We have a play to rehearse for the King. The bloody-minded, monstrous, murderous King. And you know what he does if you provoke him? Head. On. Spike. Now, let us read from the top. (*Pause.*) What?

He turns around and sees CHARLES.

Mother of God!

CHARLES. No. Just King. Look, I can see you are – practising – but if I might steal a moment with Miss Gwynn.

KILLIGREW. Of course, Your Gracious Majesty. (*To everyone.*) Out!

They begin to leave. CHARLES *addresses* NELL. NANCY *lurks, a bit of a gooseberry.*

CHARLES. You were rather good last night.

NELL. Sir.

CHARLES. Though you were better the night before.

NELL. I'm sorry?

CHARLES. You seemed distracted.

NELL. Some rogue was making eyes at me.

CHARLES. How dare he? Who does he think he is?

NELL. The King of England?!

CHARLES. So come on then. What do they pay you?

NELL. Sir!

NANCY. Two shillings.

NELL. Nan!

NANCY. But only every third night –

NELL. Hey!

NANCY. And only if it's full.

CHARLES. Scandalous! Who runs this place? We should riot! But perhaps, in the meantime, I could tempt you with a supplement.

NELL. I've given that up, sir.

CHARLES. I'd keep you well.

NELL. I don't like to be kept.

CHARLES. A hundred pounds.

NANCY. A hundred pounds!!

CHARLES. And your own lady-in-waiting.

NANCY. Hello?

NELL. I / couldn't.

CHARLES. Silks, gems, a room at the Palace. Listen. I like you.

NELL. You've only just met me.

CHARLES. You're different.

NELL. You hardly know me.

CHARLES. And I like talking to you.

NELL. And I, you.

CHARLES. A lot.

NELL. And I.

They share a moment.

CHARLES. I don't like to talk money. It does seem rather vulgar, but how much do you want?

NELL. Sir –

CHARLES. Two hundred?

NELL. I can't –

CHARLES. Two fifty?

NELL (*carefully, thinking of* HART). I have a life here… and people in it.

CHARLES. But?

NELL. There's no but, sir.

CHARLES. There was. I saw it. You caught your breath.

NELL. You misread me. I'm sorry.

CHARLES. Shame. If you're certain –

NELL. I am.

CHARLES. Then I'll leave you to your theatricals. (*Goes to leave*.) Speaking of which, have you seen Cleopatra at the Duke's? Moll Davies is mesmeric.

NELL. Moll Davies?

CHARLES. She has… 'infinite variety'.

NANCY. She should have, with her years of experience.

A stand-off.

CHARLES. Well, I must make haste. Her entrance is spectacular.

NELL. Fine.

CHARLES. Good.

NELL. Farewell.

CHARLES. That's that then.

NELL. Yes.

CHARLES. Well. Good day, Miss Gwynn. (*Exits.*)

NELL (*exploding*). Moll Davies! She's got less life in her than a leper's foot.

NANCY. Got you though, didn't it?

NELL. What?

NANCY. He's playing you.

NELL. People don't play me. How dare he! (*Pause.*) He can't – I won't let him… Nan – I need your help.

NANCY. What sort of help?

NELL. Baking.

HART *enters.* NANCY *hasn't noticed.*

NANCY. Baking? What are we baking?

NELL (*seeing* HART). Charles.

NANCY (*anticipating a scene*). I have some stockings to – try on.

NANCY *leaves. A beat.*

HART. So that's it then, is it? You and me.

NELL. –

HART. He's been here every night!

NELL. He loves the playhouse.

HART. In your dressing room.

NELL. Were you spying?

HART. Just tell me! I can take it.

NELL. There's nothing to tell. We only speak!

HART. You? Just 'speak'?!

NELL. What's that supposed to mean?

HART. Has he made you an offer?

NELL. No.

HART. You're lying.

NELL. No.

HART. Nell –

NELL. All right, yes but –

HART. But nothing! There'll be pamphlets by sunrise. The hounds don't waste a moment. Charles Hart – coxcombed in front of his public!

NELL. *Your* public?!

HART. You wouldn't even be here if I hadn't dragged you up – you'd be down in the pit, or in the alley, with your skirt around your waist and your gagging men with their grasping hands and their filthy, flaccid cocks. You were a whore!

NELL. Yes, I was. I *was*.

Beat.

HART (*fishing out some coins*). What'll you charge now? A shilling? A guinea? (*Throws them at her feet.*) I don't think I could afford you. (*Going.*)

NELL. Charlie? Charles!

HART. What?!

NELL. I turned him down. I turned him down.

HART *turns back to her, but he's blown it and he knows it.*

Scene Twelve

Laxatives

NELL *and* ROSE *are in* NELL*'s dressing room, when*
ARLINGTON *arrives*.

ARLINGTON. I'd like to speak with Miss Gwynn. Alone.

NELL. She's my sister – we have no secrets.

ARLINGTON. May I speak frankly? Your flirtation with the
    Monarch. Your supposition of his particular regard for you –

NELL. Supposition?

ARLINGTON. We won't allow it. It is – unsuitable. And if he
    comes back seeking an avenue for his pleasure –

NELL. Since when do you decide whose avenue he puts his
    pleasure in, Mr...?

ARLINGTON. *Lord*. Lord Arlington. Twentieth Baron of
    Helmsey, Foreign Secretary, Minister of Parliament and
    adviser to His Majesty. Madam, the King has a nation to
    command. You are a distraction.

NELL. What? My backstage chats with the King.

ARLINGTON. Madam, for a monarch, there is no 'backstage'.
    People talk. Tattle-tellers. Scandalmongers. There is no
    privacy when you are the King of England.

NELL. Men pay a coin to watch me change. I know about lack
    of privacy.

ARLINGTON. I don't think you understand.

NELL. You underestimate me.

ARLINGTON. We've waited a decade for him. A decade under
    the thumb of a commoner. The King is divine, madam. God's
    emissary on Earth. And you –

NELL. What? I'm a what? Go on? A commoner? A whore? You
    can't insult me, sir. I am common. And I was a whore. What
    are you scared of? That I'll bring down the English Court by
    dancing a jig in it?

ARLINGTON. You may be schooled in badinage.
    Backchatting. Tit-flirting. But your games don't wash with
    me. You will lose, so I'd strongly advise you not to play.

NELL. Are you threatening me?

ARLINGTON. I'm merely imparting friendly advice. (*Pause*.)
    How do you find it, in Coal Yard Alley?

NELL. Sir?

ARLINGTON. You hear terrible stories of girls being roughed
    up after dark. I'd hate to think you were in any danger. Not
    that anyone would notice. Round there, people just disappear
    without a trace. (*Beat*.) Good luck with the rehearsals, Miss
    Gwynn, I hope the punters are entertained.

    And with that, he is gone. NELL *is shaken.* ROSE *looks at
    her sister.*

ROSE. What are you doing?

NELL. How dare he!

ROSE. You have to stop.

NELL. Come in here?! It's my dressing room!

ROSE. He's not some sponger with a gin mouth, Nell, he's a
    courtier.

NELL. He could be Henry the Eighth for all I care, he has no
    place!

ROSE. Hey – your cheek has got you so far, but this – he's the
    King of England!

NELL. He's a man like any other.

ROSE. Nell! Walk half a mile upriver and the heads of his
    enemies are rotting on spikes!

NELL. That's political. I'm not political.

ROSE. You're a girl of no rank – a commoner. And you're a
    Protestant. Everything about you is political. They will cut
    your throat. You have to stay away from the King – you
    promise me – and if he comes back –

NANCY (*racing in*). He's here! The King is here!

ROSE. Nell, please – for once, listen to me –

CHARLES (*arriving*). Miss Gwynn. (*To* ROSE.) Trot off.

ROSE. She oughtn't to be left alone.

CHARLES. She's not alone. She's with me.

> NANCY *clears her throat*.

> And the stocking-washer.

NANCY (*sotto voce*). Wardrobe Mistress.

NELL. Go on, Rose.

> ROSE *looks at* NELL *in indignation, then leaves*.

CHARLES. Miss Gwynn. You've caused quite a scene.

NELL. 'Tis what I do, sir.

CHARLES. Don't be facetious. You've caused Miss Davies great embarrassment.

NELL. Embarrassment? What can he mean, Nancy?

NANCY. I wouldn't know, ma'am. What embarrassment, sir?

CHARLES. You know exactly what I am talking about.

NELL. No. I think you should explain.

NANCY. Oh yes, sir. Go on.

> *Pause*. CHARLES *realises he's been cornered*.

CHARLES. Last night – you caused me great dissatisfaction.

NELL. I am sorry. It's hard to satisfy a man from a mile across London. If I'd known you were alone –

CHARLES. I was in Miss Davies's company.

NANCY. Last time I heard she was in the Duke's Company, fickle wench.

CHARLES. Listen –

NELL. Couldn't she satisfy you as you'd please, sir?

CHARLES. No. She was indisposed.

NELL. Indisposed? How?

NANCY. The clap?

CHARLES. No. Laxatives.

NELL/NANCY. Laxatives?!

CHARLES. Baked into a marzipan tart.

NANCY. Well I never.

NELL. Who could have done it?

CHARLES. Nell…

NELL. How embarrassing. I hope you weren't witness to –

NANCY. Oh sir!

NELL. She didn't?!

NANCY. What? During?!

NELL. Must have put you right off.

CHARLES. You don't say.

NELL. I hope word doesn't *spread* –

NANCY. It would cause a terrible *stink* –

CHARLES. Ladies!

NELL. Sorry. We were being facetious. I mean. She was being
    'faecetious'.

    Pause.

CHARLES. You must really like me.

NELL. What makes you say that?

CHARLES. Nothing. Just being facetious. Three hundred
    pounds.

NANCY. Three hundred pounds!?

NELL. Will you make me comfortable?

CHARLES. I'll make you *very* comfortable.

    Beat.

NELL. Four hundred.

CHARLES. Four!

NELL. Call it interest.

CHARLES. Well, I do have a lot of interest. In your performance. All right. Four hundred.

NELL. And the silks.

CHARLES. And the silks.

NANCY. And the carriage.

CHARLES. And the carriage.

NELL. And the apartment.

CHARLES. What apartment?

NELL. It's an awful trek back to the Palace from Cheapside. I wouldn't want you to get your feet dirty walking home of a morning.

CHARLES. You are unbelievable.

NELL. How dare you! Haven't you seen my Florimel?

CHARLES. I've been waiting to see your Florimel for weeks. Come here.

He pulls her to him. They see NANCY *watching. He indicates that she should turn round to face the wall, which she does.*

Well. If you are to have the silks –

NELL. And the carriage –

NANCY. And the apartment –

NELL. And five hundred pounds –

CHARLES. Five?! Five. Then I shall want to see you all the time.

NELL. Whenever you like.

CHARLES. Shall I come often?

NELL. Every night.

CHARLES. Every night?

NELL. Maybe even twice.

They kiss.

Scene Thirteen

Territory

At the Palace. NELL *is moving into* LADY CASTLEMAINE*'s apartments.* SERVANTS *move luggage and furniture to and fro.* NELL *watches in awe. Two* SERVANTS, WILLIAM *and another, carry a grand-looking chest.*

WILLIAM. Where shall we put this, ma'am?

NELL. What is it?

WILLIAM. A Byzantine urn of Istrian marble, from the ancient Court of Constantine the Great.

NELL. Is that what they call it?

LADY CASTLEMAINE (*appearing*). I find it sits well on the terrace. It catches the afternoon light.

NELL (*curtseying*). Lady Castlemaine.

LADY CASTLEMAINE (*to the* SERVANTS). Be gone.

The SERVANTS *don't move.*

Didn't you hear me?

WILLIAM. Miss Gwynn?

NELL. Thank you, William.

WILLIAM *exits.*

I thought you'd left last night.

LADY CASTLEMAINE. I decided to stay. I wanted to meet you. I've never met an actress before.

NELL. And?

LADY CASTLEMAINE. You're just as I imagined. I wonder what he sees in you. They say you've the voice of a linnet. Go on, little bird. Sing.

NELL. I don't perform on demand.

LADY CASTLEMAINE. Oh dear, then you won't last long with the King. Go on. Entertain me.

NELL pauses. She decides to improvise a song.

NELL (*singing*).
> Long live Lady Castlemaine,
> Some folk call her Barb-ra.
> Every man in Eng-a-land
> Follows her hereafter.
> Every gent from here to Kent,
> Longing for her ardour.
> For she's mum to all of 'em!
> And nobody knows their father.
> Long live Lady Castlemaine,
> Or should I call you Barb'ra,
> Every man in Eng-a-land
> Will follow her hereafter.

Pause.

LADY CASTLEMAINE. That is sweet.

NELL (*singing*).
> Fairest Lady Castlemaine
> Has many fine admirers.
> Each, when she is tired of him,
> Conveniently expires.
> Now the King tires of her thing
> And she has lost her splendour.
> Flew to close to the candle flame
> And ended her day as an ember!

LADY CASTLEMAINE. My dear, I chose to leave. I'm going to France.

NELL. And what's in France?

LADY CASTLEMAINE. Louis. Of course. May I offer some
advice?

NELL. I can make my own way.

LADY CASTLEMAINE. That's what you think. I'm afraid you
have the glow.

NELL. And what's the glow?

LADY CASTLEMAINE. You're flushed. You feel chosen,
don't you? Special. And you are – for a while. But it won't
last. And when he tires of you, as he will, he'll spit you out
and throw you back whence you came. Only you can't go
back. Because everything you had, you've given up. For
him. You will be lost. Sunk.

NELL. I have to unpack.

LADY CASTLEMAINE. Good day, Miss Gwynn. One more
thing. Claim your title before your body's wracked in
childbirth.

NELL. I don't want a title.

LADY CASTLEMAINE. I'm sorry?

NELL. You think that's why I'm here?

LADY CASTLEMAINE. Why else are you here?

NELL. I'm not like you. I don't want to be a lady. Or a duchess.
I don't want any of that.

LADY CASTLEMAINE. Then why… (*Pause*.) Oh dear God.
You love him. You're in love with the King. You poor,
impotent child. Well. Then there's nothing in the world can
help you now.

LADY CASTLEMAINE *leaves*. NELL *watches her go,
shaken…*

End of Act One.

ACT TWO

Scene One

At the Palace

A good few years later…

CHARLES *is late for a morning meeting with* ARLINGTON.

ARLINGTON. You're late.

CHARLES. I was washing my wig.

ARLINGTON *gives him a sarcastic look.*

What? There's a lot of it.

ARLINGTON. Here are the treaties.

CHARLES. I'll read them later.

ARLINGTON. They need signing today.

CHARLES. I'll look at them after my – other activities.

ARLINGTON. Enlighten me?

CHARLES. I'm playing piquet with Nell. Then walking the dogs.

ARLINGTON. Again.

CHARLES. It's for their health, Arley. No one likes a fat dog. Besides, people like to see me with the spaniels. It's becoming a bit of a thing.

ARLINGTON. They need signing today.

CHARLES. It's Sunday. Don't you have church to go to?

ARLINGTON. Don't you?

CHARLES. When I go to Mass, the Protestants whinge. When I go to chapel, the Catholics moan. I can't win, so I vote – stay in bed. Besides, the priest's taken against me; whenever I go for confession, he darts out the door.

ARLINGTON. Last time you went to confession it took eight-and-a-half hours.

CHARLES. What can I say? (*Proudly.*) 'Forgive me, Father, for I have sinned – A LOT!' I'm going to have to do some serious flirting at the pearly gates.

ARLINGTON. You know it wouldn't harm French relations for you to attend the odd Mass while they're here.

CHARLES. That's a week away.

ARLINGTON. They're coming today.

CHARLES. What?! I thought they were coming on the second.

ARLINGTON. It is the second.

CHARLES. That blasted sundial. I shouldn't read it when I'm drunk.

ARLINGTON (*suddenly exploding*). Does it ever cross your mind that your seat is under threat?! You have no heir, your brother's threatening to convert, the Puritans hate you, the Catholics hate you, the Dutch are burning our ships, the Spanish are up in arms, we've lost three colonies in the last fortnight and you're gadding about with your spaniels. And with *her*. The nation's falling apart! Don't you care?

CHARLES. Of course I care! What do you want me to do about it?

ARLINGTON. You're the King! You've not made a single decision for weeks, other than to run us dry, frittering the funds on your oversized playhouses!

CHARLES. Playhouses are a valuable national asset.

ARLINGTON. Oh, very good, we get marks for poncing about in funny hats while being systematically scrubbed off the map. You'll be remembered for bringing back theatre and leaving the country in tatters.

CHARLES. What's the point of having a country if it's sapped of all joy, Arlington? Down with austerity!

ARLINGTON. Parliament's accusing you of sitting on the fence. They say you're weak. You have to take a stand.

CHARLES. You really are a fool, Arlington.

ARLINGTON. Sir!

CHARLES. Do you honestly think I've let things drift because I can't be bothered? I'm sitting on the fence because it's the only way to survive. Every signature I leave is like inking my own death warrant. Have you forgotten what happened to my father? I've no intention of signing those. Not one of them. And you can ask me till the dogs have been walked and the cows come home, I'm not signing a damned thing. Maybe my legacy will be one of indecision, maybe. But it's the only way to keep my head. What else can I do? (*Beat.*) And *that* is why I'm seeing my Nell.

He goes to exit.

ARLINGTON. Sir?

CHARLES. What?

ARLINGTON. Humour me for a moment.

CHARLES. Oh no.

ARLINGTON. Our alliance with France –

CHARLES. I knew it.

ARLINGTON. We need them to trust us.

CHARLES. Can't we just send them a gift?

ARLINGTON. Like what?

CHARLES. Tennis balls?

ARLINGTON. Sir. Our bond with them is fragile. We need to forge a link, a 'relationship' if you will. They've brought a lady with them.

CHARLES. I have my Nelly.

ARLINGTON. They call her the 'Belle Dame'.

CHARLES. Arlington.

ARLINGTON. She's exquisite –

CHARLES. No.

ARLINGTON. *Gentile* –

CHARLES. No.

ARLINGTON. And constantly libidinous. (*Pause.*) Just – talk to her. Take her for a turn.

CHARLES. I will not take another mistress.

ARLINGTON. Fine. (*Pause.*) They say she has the stamina of a wild boar.

CHARLES looks at ARLINGTON. NELL *arrives with two beautiful cloaks.*

NELL. Charles. Crimson or buff? It's for Newmarket. I think – (*Picking the buff.*) this one. (*About the crimson.*) I wore this at Richmond last spring, and I'd rather not give the pamphleteers the satisfaction of pointing it out. (*Looking at them both.*) What?

ARLINGTON. Just think about it.

CHARLES (*purposefully ignoring him*). Buff. I like you best in the buff. (*To* ARLINGTON.) Are you still here?

ARLINGTON. I shall go and make arrangements. (*Exits.*)

CHARLES. Arlington!

But he's gone.

NELL. What arrangements?

CHARLES. It's nothing. The French are coming, that's all.

NELL. I thought as much. They're all in a tizz in the kitchens. They spent all night dredging the ponds for frogs, then the boy let them loose in the larder. You look tired. Is Arlington tormenting you? Shall I set Kynaston on him?

CHARLES. Come here.

He pulls her too him. They share a tender moment. He runs his fingers through her hair.

Your hair is different.

NELL. I've got a new woman. She rolls it in paper.

CHARLES. I like it. It suits you.

NELL. Thanks.

She kisses him then looks at him with concern.

Charlie?

CHARLES. It's nothing. Just France. We're on a knife-edge with them.

NELL. You'll charm them. You always do. What's he asking of you?

CHARLES. Arlington? Too much.

NELL. He's pushy – he's a Catholic. But he's nobody's fool. Maybe you should listen to him.

CHARLES. You can't stand him!

NELL. I can't bear him. But he's clever. And if he wants you to befriend them, it's probably for good reason.

CHARLES. Hm. And as if that's not enough, my blockhead of a brother is threatening to join the Papists. Catholics?! Really! Do you think he does it to vex me?

NELL. Course he does. Lord knows, there's precious little advantage to being the younger. You got the crown, and this old place. At least let him have a little fun.

CHARLES. But Popery?! We'll never hear the end of it.

She kisses him.

NELL. You've got too much in your head. You haven't slept. Hey, I've got a game'll cheer you up.

CHARLES. Hunt the royal sausage?

NELL. Not after where you hid it last time.

CHARLES. It was dark.

NELL. Let's play 'Guess the Mistress'.

CHARLES. Oh please, no!

NELL. You love it when I dress up.

CHARLES. I love it when you undress.

She heads for the door and, as she does, she wraps herself in the cloaks and imitates Lady Castlemaine.

NELL. 'Charlie! Charlie! Make me a duchess!'

CHARLES. Or what?

NELL. 'Or I shall elope with the Duke of Marlborough and leave you with a monumental bill, a gaggle of bastard children and a very itchy sceptre.'

CHARLES. Good day, Barbara Castlemaine.

NELL. Very good. (*Feigning a dramatic posture and an 'actory' voice.*) 'Charlie! Darling Charlie. I need you. I need you like a piglet needs a teat, I need you like a loony needs a leech, I need – oh – oh dear – I need a bucket!'

CHARLES. Begone, Moll Davies!

NELL. Too late! Did I splash you?

CHARLES. You know she never forgave you.

NELL (*preparing for the next impression*). Ready –

CHARLES. Nell, shouldn't you be at the theatre?

NELL. Oh come on, I thought you wanted to play hunt the sausage. (*Exits.*)

CHARLES. All right then! (*Follows.*)

ROSE *and her mother,* OLD MA GWYNN, *enter, accompanied by* WILLIAM, *the servant.*

WILLIAM. Ah. She was here, madam.

ROSE. Well, can you fetch her? It's important.

WILLIAM. Ma'am. (*Exits.*)

MA GWYNN. Would you look at that! (*About the room.*) It's as pretty as a petticoat. I have never seen such a very big pillar in all my life.

ROSE. Mother, don't touch anything.

MA GWYNN. It's here. The spirit of Madame Geneva. I can smell it.

ROSE. Please. Just – where are you going?!

MA GWYNN. I can feel it – barrels of it!

WILLIAM *returns with* NELL, *who is flustered. He exits.*

NELL. Rose! What are you doing here?

ROSE. We came to see you.

NELL. We?

MA GWYNN (*off*). Now if I was a gin jar, where would I think I'd be?

NELL. Mother.

MA GWYNN. My Nelly! Look at you, you little blue blood. Let me have a proper look. My squirrel, who'd have thought it, eh? My little Nell, all in silk.

NELL. Ma.

MA GWYNN. You are like a jewel my girl. Your hair. Is that a wiggle on your head?

NELL. A wig. No, it's just been curled. My girl does it for me.

MA GWYNN. You have a girl? Well, I never. My girl has a girl! I hardly recognise you.

NELL. You didn't tell me you were coming.

MA GWYNN. I'm your mother, I don't need an appointment.

NELL. I was with the King. You really ought to –

ROSE. We haven't seen you for months –

NELL. I'm sorry. But I am meant to be at rehearsals.

MA GWYNN. 'S all right, we'll dally here till you get back, my duck. Just get me a drop of gin. (*Goes off in search of the gin.*) A spirit for me spirits, a tipple for me tickle.

NELL *pulls* ROSE *to one side to talk to her out of earshot.*

ROSE. You see what she's like, Nell?!

NELL. Did anyone see you come?

ROSE. Why?

NELL. You can't just turn up here. This is Court.

ROSE. Are you embarrassed by us?

NELL. No.

ROSE. I hope not.

NELL. Of course I'm not, but you can't just tramp in like –

MA GWYNN (*arriving back in the conversation unexpectedly*). Like what? Like a madam from the brothel?

NELL. Yes, like a madam from the brothel.

MA GWYNN. Charming.

NELL. Ma, I've sent you coins!

MA GWYNN. Oh, how kind of you to remember us in your alms for the poor.

NELL. You're not even grateful! Why won't you let me help you? I've paid your way out.

MA GWYNN. You think I ought to give it up? Nelly. I built that house from nothing, from sot and spit. And it pays my way. And all without a fella. Who else can say that, Nelly? Not you.

NELL. If you knew how they judge me –

ROSE. How they judge you?!

NELL. I've made my name –

MA GWYNN. As what? You're no different from the rest of my girls. You're the same as you always were, you're just a more expensive whore.

NELL. I have an allowance for support – it's not the same.

MA GWYNN. 'It's not the same'?!

NELL. It isn't!

MA GWYNN. You're right, it's not. Cos my girls aren't ashamed of who they are. They tell the truth. They don't try and scrape it away like a scab on the skin, paint over it with all your fine unctions and paste. It'll crack, Nell. By God, I'd rather you're a slattern than a liar who denies her own kind.

NELL. Why did you come here? If I'm such a disappointment.

MA GWYNN. Oh, you're not. I'm proud of you. It lights up my heart when I think of what you've done. It's just who you are that I can't bear.

OLD MA GWYNN *leaves, followed by* ROSE.

NELL. Rose, please!

ROSE. I've asked you again and again to come home. And you haven't! What could I do but bring her here?

NELL. What can *I* do? I have responsibilities! I've sent you coins.

ROSE. She's steeped in it. And I can't cope. Not on my own. You have to help me.

NELL. She doesn't deserve it.

ROSE. She's your mother.

NELL. And what's she done for me?

ROSE. You owe her everything.

NELL. I owe her nothing. Everything I've done's in spite of her.

ROSE. Your pluck to get on the boards. Where d'you get that? The way you talk to a man and wind him in. Your cheek and quip. She taught you how to sell. To scrap. To make your way. And now she's drowning in it. And you can hardly look at her. Please, Nelly.

NELL. I'll come home.

ROSE. You will? You promise.

NELL. Yes.

ROSE. Nelly.

NELL. Yes – I do.

ROSE. When?

NELL. Soon –

ROSE. When?

NELL. Tomorrow. I'll come tomorrow.

ROSE *looks at her. Exeunt.*

Scene Two

Emergency Meeting

Later the same day. All the COMPANY *are assembled.* NELL *is late.*

KILLIGREW. We're facing a crisis.

NED. What crisis?

NANCY. The Duke's are opening a new playhouse.

KYNASTON. What?!

HART. Where?

NANCY. At Whitefriars!

NED. But they'll close us down!

KILLIGREW. Thank you for stating the obvious, Ned. We need a plan. A hit. And we need to sell out. And there's only one way to guarantee a sell-out.

HART. Nell.

KYNASTON. Just for a change.

KILLIGREW. She sells tickets, Edward. So I've trawled theatrical history, from the classics to the long forgotten, in search of a play with a brilliant female lead.

NANCY. Good for you! And what have you found?

KILLIGREW. Nothing.

NED. Nothing?

NANCY. Not one single play, out of every play that's ever been written?

KILLIGREW. No. Oh they're all splendid works, epic adventures, but not one has a half-decent lead for a lady. There's nothing for it, we'll have to revive *The Enchanted Island*.

HART. But we already revived it – twice!

KILLIGREW. And they loved her in it.

NANCY. But all the palm trees have wilted.

HART. Killigrew, please – it's just lobsters and fish jokes and Ned mincing about as a mermaid.

NED. Hey!

KILLIGREW. But it sells! I hate to remind you 'artistes', but I am trying to run a business here. The Duke's don't open for a fortnight and already they're selling out!

NED. What are they doing?

KILLIGREW. *King Lear* – the comedy.

DRYDEN. *King Lear* isn't funny.

KILLIGREW. It is now. No one dies and it's got a happy ending. We must compete or we'll go under. It's either that, or Dryden writes a new play.

DRYDEN. But I've dried up.

KILLIGREW. Just write anything – as long as Nell's in it.

NANCY. She's the heroine, write her a lover's part.

NED. She's funny, write her a comic part.

KYNASTON. She's a woman, write her a tit part.

DRYDEN. Does anyone care what I want to write?

ALL. No!

KILLIGREW. People want jokes.

DRYDEN. But I've used them all up. It's not easy being a massive success. The weight of expectation on my shoulders... I'm like Atlas.

KILLIGREW. Oh, for God's sake.

DRYDEN. Unless... Wait! I've got it!

KILLIGREW. It's about a woman?

DRYDEN. Yes. Yes it is. We're in Denmark. There's a Prince – ess.

KILLIGREW. Dryden!

DRYDEN. Oh! Or how about... 'Juliet'!

NANCY. What, on her own?

DRYDEN. Why not?

KILLIGREW. It might be a bit thin in terms of story arc. Girl meets no one, nothing happens!

DRYDEN. All right, all right. How about... this! There's a rich girl. And she's betrothed to a heartless nobleman. Then one day, she meets a pauper. And they fall wildly in love.

NED. Ooh. Where?

DRYDEN. On a journey. On horseback.

KILLIGREW. No more animals. Not after what happened with the snakes.

DRYDEN. All right... on a galleon.

ALL. Ooh... Yes!

DRYDEN. Sailing across the Atlantic. And then, out of nowhere... there's a giant trout!

Pause.

Or – a rock!

NANCY. Why would there be a rock?

DRYDEN. Wait! An iceberg!

ALL. Ooh!

DRYDEN. And the galleon hits the iceberg, and splits in twain, and the pauper boy drowns!

Beat.

NANCY. That is the stupidest idea I have ever heard.

KILLIGREW. No tragedy. No drowning. We need drama. They want battles, swords and shields, and Nell.

KYNASTON. How's that going to work?

KILLIGREW. I don't know! All I know is the more she's in it, and the more we see of her... wait! Lady Godiva!

HART. Lady Godiva?

NELL (*arriving*). Lady who?

DRYDEN. There you are.

KILLIGREW. You're late.

KYNASTON. Again.

NELL. It's mayhem out there. The French have arrived and they're all driving on the wrong side of the cobbles.

KILLIGREW. You were meant to be here at noon.

NELL. I'm sorry.

HART. We've heard that before.

NELL *looks at* HART *and decides to ignore him.*

NELL. I heard about the Duke's. What'll we do?

KILLIGREW. Survive – with our brand new hit.

DRYDEN. Nell, how would you like to play the boldest beacon in English history?

NELL. Who? Queen Elizabeth?

DRYDEN. No... Lady Godiva!

NELL. Who?

DRYDEN. She was a warrior.

KILLIGREW. A heroine. The most valiant woman to ride on English soil.

NELL. Perfect. So who was she?

They all look at each other.

Come on, what did she fight for?

KILLIGREW. Well... she... she fought for...

DRYDEN. ...things, against...

KILLIGREW. ...people.

DRYDEN. She is ever so important.

NELL. Who'd she fight?

KILLIGREW. Dryden?

DRYDEN. I don't quite remember.

KILLIGREW. Nor I. It didn't seem to feature much in the story.

NELL. And what is the story? She's got to be famous for something.

KILLIGREW. Well, because...

DRYDEN. Because...

NANCY. Because she got her tits out. She's famous for getting her tits out.

NED. In Coventry.

NELL. And that's it, is it?

Silence. NELL *is mortified.*

Thank you very much.

DRYDEN. Nell, don't be like that.

NELL. Like what? All you know is that she showed her chest. And that's enough to build a play on, is it?

KYNASTON. You'd be surprised.

DRYDEN. Please, Nell.

NELL. No.

KILLIGREW. We need you.

NELL. No.

NED. But you're Nell Gwynn!

DRYDEN. And they love what you do.

HART. It's not what she does, it's *who* she does.

Pause.

NELL. Sorry?

HART. That's why they come.

Everyone looks at him.

What? Everyone knows it. It's just none of you have the groats to say it. They don't give two figs about your performance. They just want to see the King's mistress.

NELL. That's not true. (*Pause.*) Dryden?

DRYDEN. Definitely not. I mean, a bit.

NELL. Ned?

NED looks away.

Thomas?

KILLIGREW. It's not just that, of course.

DRYDEN. We need you. Please?

NELL. No.

CHARLES *arrives with a veiled woman,* LOUISE DE KEROUALLE, *with a parasol, accompanied by a royal* ATTENDANT. *The rest of the* COMPANY *sees, except* NELL *and* KILLIGREW.

NANCY. Nell!

NELL. No.

NED. Nell!

NELL. I said no. (*From their looks*.) What?

NELL *turns round and sees* CHARLES, *who is standing behind* KILLIGREW.

Oh.

KILLIGREW (*spinning round to see* CHARLES). Jesus Christ!

CHARLES. Close enough.

NELL. Who's this? Hamlet's father?

CHARLES. This is Madame de Keroualle. She is my guest.

LOUISE DE KEROUALLE *lifts her veil*. NELL *is horrified to see the beauty underneath*.

NELL. Oh.

LOUISE. *Bonjour*.

NELL. How do you do?

CHARLES. She doesn't speak English.

NELL. Well, that's convenient.

CHARLES. I'm just showing her around. She asked to see my theatre. *Louise, je vous présente Eleanor Gwynn*. [Louise, this lady is Eleanor Gwynn.]

LOUISE. *Enchantée*. [Thrilled.]

NELL. Yep.

CHARLES. Nell is the darling of the English stage, *la belle dame du théâtre anglais*.

LOUISE. *Elle est comédienne?* [She is an actress?]

CHARLES. *La meilleure*. [The best.]

LOUISE. *Ah, c'est différent en Angleterre. En France, toutes les comédiennes sont des prostituées*. [Oh, it's different in England. In France, all the actresses are prostitutes.]

NELL. Excuse me?

LOUISE. *Je peux assister à une représentation?* [May I come to a performance?]

CHARLES. *Bien sûr!* [Of course.] She'd like to come to a play. We'll come on Saturday.

KILLIGREW. Sir, that would be marvellous.

NELL *looks at* KILLIGREW *with incredulity.*

LOUISE. *Je me ferai faire un chapeau tout spécialement. Je vais commander un tissu de Paris. Je serai magnifique.* [I will have a hat made especially. I will order fabric from Paris. I will be splendid.]

CHARLES. But first I might show her the Shires. Oxford perhaps. I might take her for a punt.

NELL. I took her for a punt as soon as I set eyes on her.

CHARLES (*pulling her to one side*). Nell, it's just 'international relations'. You know the arrangement.

NELL. You brought her *here*?

A stand-off.

I thought you were leaving for Oxford.

CHARLES. I was hoping you would come.

NELL. You were?

CHARLES. We'll overnight at Windsor and be back on Wednesday.

HART. But we have to rehearse, sir.

CHARLES. Ah. Then next time.

NELL. No! I'll come.

DRYDEN. But my play!

CHARLES. She doesn't need to practise. She's a natural.

LOUISE *sneezes.*

À tes souhaits. [Bless you.]

NELL. What's wrong with her?

CHARLES. She has a delicate constitution.

NELL. So do we, Charles. I assumed that's why she's here.

CHARLES. Nell…

Pause. Awkward.

LOUISE. *Charlie! On y va!* [Charlie! Let's go!]

CHARLES. I'll send a carriage for you. I hope you will behave.
(*To all.*) Good day.

CHARLES *and* LOUISE *exit. A pause.*

HART. Tell me you're not going to allow this.

KILLIGREW. Not now, Mr Hart.

HART. Not now?! She can't just swan up at the prologue. We
have to rehearse – together. We're supposed to be a company.

KYNASTON. We always used to be.

KILLIGREW. He's the King. What could I say?

HART. She chose him!

NANCY. She doesn't have a choice.

HART. She could have said no.

DRYDEN. What about my play?

KILLIGREW. I don't know?! I don't know! We don't even
have a plan, if Lady Godiva's been vetoed –

NELL. I'll do it.

KILLIGREW. What?

NELL. I'll play her.

NANCY. You can't!

NELL. I'll do it.

NANCY. She's a tart – on a horse!

NELL. I'm an actress, Nan. It's what I do. I'll play the part. I
need some air.

NANCY. Allow the lady some room. Now!

DRYDEN (*going*). Thanks, Nell!

The COMPANY *exits at pace.* NANCY, *realising the problem, brings a bucket.* NELL *throws up in it.*

NANCY. How long have you known?

NELL. A month. Maybe more.

NANCY. Why didn't you tell me?

NELL. I hoped I could wish it away. I've seen what happens, you're fresh and spruce and he can't keep away, but once a baby comes...

NANCY. You're different, he said.

NELL. He brought her here, Nan! To the playhouse.

Pause.

NANCY. It might not mean..

NELL. You saw how he looked at her.

NANCY. I don't know.

NELL. Nancy.

NANCY *doesn't say anything. She knows.* LOUISE *reappears.*

LOUISE. *Pardon. J'ai oublié mon parasol. Vous l'avez vu?* (*Pause.*) *Non? Imbéciles.* [Sorry, I forgot my parasol. Have you seen it? No? Imbeciles.]

NELL *and* NANCY *say nothing.* LOUISE *looks round the theatre with distaste.*

NELL. Must be hard for her, not knowing what they're saying behind her back – about her spying and her whoring. I almost feel sorry for her.

LOUISE. I do not need your sympathy.

NELL (*caught out*). Oh.

LOUISE. But I have learnt the English. In case I am asked to stay here. In London.

NELL. And how do you like London?

LOUISE. I don't.

NELL. Then go home.

LOUISE. It's impossible. It would not please to the King.

NELL. And you know how to please him, do you?

LOUISE. I see how it is here. Your men pay.

NELL. Your men don't. So who's the fool now?

LOUISE. If you were loved, he would not pay.

NELL (*taken aback*). That's not true. I had him first.

LOUISE. It must be sad for you that, to him, you were not
enough. *Il se peut bien que vous soyez comédienne, mais je
vais vous voler la vedette si c'est la dernière chose que je
ferai. Ce soir-là, je mettrai un chapeau tellement
spectaculaire que vous aurez l'air d'une merde à la semelle
de ma chaussure. Bonne journée.* [You may be an actress,
but I will upstage you if it's the last thing I do. On the night,
I will wear a hat so spectacular that it'll make you look like a
shit on the sole of my shoe. Good day.]

LOUISE *goes. Pause.*

NELL. What in hell's name was that?!

NANCY. Well, first she said though you're an actress, she'll
upstage you if it's the last thing she does, then she said she'll
have a hat made so spectacular that it'll make you look like a
shit on the sole of her shoe. And then she said – have a nice
day.

NELL. Nancy!

NANCY. Yep, once I had a thing with Molière's dresser.

NELL. The spiteful dog. There's only one thing for it.

NANCY. War.

NELL. With France.

Scene Three

War with the French

Opening night. Fanfare. CHARLES *and* LOUISE *appear in the Royal Box.* LOUISE *removes her cloak to reveal an embellished hat the size of a cartwheel. The crowd go wild for it.*
ARLINGTON *looks on, delighted by this 'special' relationship. There's commotion offstage, and a reluctant* NED *is pushed on.*

NED. Your Majesty. Madame. Gentles.
    Tonight, before we tell a tale of our Great British Island,
    We bring you un aperitif that we hope will beguile – and
    In honour of our guest royale who's come ashore from distant France,
    Our heroine, one Nelly Gwynn, will dedicate a song and dance.

A figure arrives on stage, to a musical crescendo, wearing a hat so enormous that we can hardly see her at all. It's a homemade replica of LOUISE*'s wide-brimmed hat, but about four times the size. At the swell of the music,* NELL *lifts the brim to reveal her face and curtsies to the Royal Box. Her whole outfit is a comic exaggeration of* LOUISE*'s.* LOUISE *is mortified. The audience is delighted.* NELL *does a little mime act, pretending to be mortally offended that she has the same outfit as* LOUISE*. The music strikes up.* NELL *sings with a fake French accent.*

NELL (*singing*).
    Bonjour, bonne journée
    Ecoutez-moi, je parle français!
    Pas d'anglais, s'il vous plaît!
    J'aime le vin de Beaujolais.
    J'aime un bol de crème brûlée.
    J'aime le goût de frais soufflé,
    Mais plus que tout, mais plus que tout,
    J'aime votre Roi! Enchantée!

    Je suis arrivée par bateau.
    Aimez-vous mon grand chapeau?
    Votre Roi est vraiment beau.
    Il m'achèt'ra un gros château!

Charlie est le plus grand Roi.
Voulez vous coucher ce soir avec moi?
Mais plus que tout, mais plus que tout,
J'aime votre Roi! Enchantée!

Translation for guidance only.

[Good morning, good day.
Listen to me, I'm speaking French!
No English, thank you!
I love wine from Beaujolais.
I love a bowl of crème brulee.
I love the taste of fresh soufflé.
But more than that, more than that,
I love your King! My pleasure!

I arrived on a boat.
Do you like my enormous hat?
Your King is really handsome.
He's going to buy me a big castle!
Charlie is the greatest King.
Will you have sex with me tonight?
But more than that, more than that,
I love your King! My pleasure!]

LOUISE *stands up and leaves the Royal Box in a huff.*

Oh! You didn't think she was me? That she was me and I
was she? No ladies, gentles, Your Majesty – I am the
Protestant whore!

Laughter and applause. NELL *does a little jig.* CHARLES
*shouldn't approve, but he does. At the end of it she bows and
the crowd go wild.* ARLINGTON *is fuming.* NELL *is
triumphant.*

Scene Four

Too Far

Moments later, NELL *arrives in the dressing room, to find* ARLINGTON *waiting for her.*

ARLINGTON. I warned you not to interfere.

NELL. It's sixpence to watch.

ARLINGTON. Do you have any sense of what you've done?

NELL (*undressing, to* NANCY). Help me with this.

ARLINGTON. Everything we've worked for hangs by a thread and then you humiliate her – and him –

NELL. It was a joke!

ARLINGTON. There are no jokes in politics. There are consequences.

NELL. And I didn't humiliate him. I sang a ditty!

ARLINGTON. There are forces at work, decisions being made that you know nothing of. The future of this nation is at stake, and I'll do whatever it takes to protect it.

ROSE *has arrived.*

NELL. My sister's here. You might want to get out of her way.

ARLINGTON. And that's all you've got to say, is it?

NELL. What do you want, an apology?

ARLINGTON. You've gone too far.

NELL. You can't hurt me, sir.

ARLINGTON. Hm. (*To* ROSE.) Madam. (*Exits.*)

ROSE. What was that?

NELL. I didn't know you were in.

ROSE. I wasn't. You said you'd come home.

NELL. Oh, Rosey, not now –

ROSE. You promised me.

NELL. I've been busy! I have duties.

ROSE. Of course. Parading at Court and fucking the King.

NELL (*taken aback*). Rose! It's not easy; I have
responsibilities –

ROSE. Not easy? You have five hundred pounds a year to do as
you please.

NELL. The five hundred pounds comes with obligations.

ROSE. An apartment at the Palace. A house on Pall Mall. You
want for nothing while the rest of us crawl around in the
Alley where you left us.

NELL. I have to work to keep in favour, Rose, I'm not the new
girl any more. And I'm with child! If he decided that was it,
I'd be out on my own again.

ROSE. Well, I feel for you.

NELL. I've given you money. And her money. I've kept Mother
from ruin.

ROSE. By sending your woman with coins that she spends on
drink? Nell! At least when she had none, she sometimes
stopped drinking.

NELL. I can't just turn up in Coal Yard Alley in dresses the
King's bought me. I'd be torn apart.

ROSE. You could have worn something different.

NELL. I'm a member of Court!

ROSE. She's your mother.

NELL. I'll go home. I'll go and see her.

ROSE. She's dead.

NELL. –

ROSE. They found her in a pond in Vauxhall; think she'd lost
her way and was so gin-soaked that she fell. She couldn't
swim, even without the drink. They brought her back last
night. Swollen. I hardly recognised her. She had reeds in her
hair. You'd think –

So it's too late. I thought you should know. We'll bury her next week.

NELL. Let me. I'll arrange it. Let me / pay.

ROSE. Listen to yourself. We won't be needing your help. If you can find time between your responsibilities, you might turn up.

Scene Five

Players or Patron

DRYDEN *sits scribbling.* NELL *turns up carrying a floral headdress and her role. She is deflated by her mother's death.* DRYDEN *doesn't notice.*

NELL. Dryden –

DRYDEN. Wait! (*Scribbling.*)

NELL. John –

DRYDEN. Nothing rhymes with Godiva. Except driver. Or diver – that's no good – unless I set it at the seaside.

NELL. Dryden, please.

DRYDEN. Wait!

Pause.

NELL. Survivor. Survivor rhymes with Godiva.

DRYDEN. Genius!

He goes back to scribbling. She holds up the garland.

NELL. What's this?

DRYDEN. Flowers?

NELL. Apparently it's my costume. All of it.

DRYDEN. Ah. Well –

NELL. I said I'd play her bare breasted.

DRYDEN. Now / about that…

NELL. 'Godiva enters naked, but for a floral wreath.'

DRYDEN. You're worried they'll notice you're swelling?

NELL. It's not what we agreed!

DRYDEN. Well, it's really a matter for Killigrew. Ask him at rehearsal.

NELL. I can't stay for rehearsal.

DRYDEN. But we're doing the final act!

KILLIGREW *enters. He's been looking for* NELL.

KILLIGREW. Ah, / Nell –

NELL. We need to talk about this. (*Holding the garland up.*) I won't do it. I won't wear it.

KILLIGREW. No, I don't suppose you will.

NELL. Sorry?

KILLIGREW. You haven't quite complicated things enough. You have to compromise this play too.

NELL. You're asking me to go on naked!

KILLIGREW. It would hardly be out of character.

NELL (*bewildered*). Have I missed something?

KILLIGREW. Yes, Nell. Rehearsals.

NELL. I've learnt the lines.

KILLIGREW. And shamed us with your tawdry song.

NELL. It was in jest!

KILLIGREW. We can't afford to be political.

NELL. We're not!

KILLIGREW. We are when you insult the French on our stage.

NELL. It's only what they're saying out there already.

KILLIGREW. What's that got to do with anything?

NELL. We're their voice! And if not that, then what are we?
(*Holding up the garland*.) A tuppenny fairground peep show? I
can speak, Dryden, for God's sake give me something to say.

KILLIGREW. You insulted the King's mistress.

NELL. I am the King's mistress!

KILLIGREW. I know. And it's too much.

NELL. I can manage it.

KILLIGREW. For us, Nell. It's too much for us. I will not put
us through this any more.

Pause.

NELL. Sir, please.

KILLIGREW. I've made up my mind.

DRYDEN. Thomas – what are you saying?

KILLIGREW. A man came from the Palace.

NELL. Arlington.

KILLIGREW. He said he'd watch us burn.

NELL. They're empty threats.

KILLIGREW. I'm afraid you're out of the company.

DRYDEN. She's our finest actor, even Hart doesn't match her.

KILLIGREW. He was good once! Before she broke him.

NELL. You taught me, sir. I worked so hard. Please, this is what
I want.

DRYDEN. More than the King?

NELL. John!

DRYDEN. If she gave him up. If she left the Palace – for us.
Would you let her stay?

KILLIGREW. I don't know.

NELL. But I love the King.

DRYDEN. You're my muse.

NELL. Sir, don't force me to choose. Please. (*Pause*.) Please?

At that moment, HART *bursts in carrying* ROSE *in his arms like a broken doll.* NANCY *and* NED *accompany.*

HART. Clear a space!

NELL. Rose!

NANCY. Nell – quickly –

NELL. What have they done?!

KILLIGREW. God in Heaven.

NED. We found her outside the theatre.

HART. Her breathing's short. Help me.

They put her down. NELL *kneels down to tend to her, she wipes the blood from* ROSE*'s face with her hands.*

NELL. Rose? Rosey?

KILLIGREW. Did you see anyone?

HART. The street was deserted.

NED. They'd propped her in the doorway.

NANCY. They meant us to find her.

KILLIGREW. Empty threats, Nell? Not political? Really?!

Scene Six

Nell and Charles

At the Palace. CHARLES is reading a letter. NELL enters, bloodied from the previous scene.

NELL. Charles?

CHARLES (*without looking up*). Look at this – another motion against my brother. Really! He may be a Catholic – and a liability – but he is the rightful heir. But will they hear it? Ugh! How was the play?

NELL. –

CHARLES. Good audience?

NELL. We didn't go on.

CHARLES. What? (*Noticing that she's blood-spotted.*) Good God, are you hurt?

NELL. It's not my blood.

CHARLES. What happened?!

NELL. They almost killed her.

CHARLES. Who?

NELL. Rose. He said from the start, if I came here – if I – but I never thought – not to her!

CHARLES. Who did?

NELL. Arlington.

CHARLES. Arlington! Where is she? Is she safe?

NELL. Yes, now. But if we hadn't found her –

CHARLES. Nelly. What can I do?

NELL. It's my fault.

CHARLES. We'll have a room prepared. My physician will attend.

NELL. Thank you, but I'm taking her home.

CHARLES. She should be near you.

NELL. And she will be. I'm going with her.

CHARLES. To Cheapside?! For how long? (*Pause*.) Nell?!

NELL. I'm sorry –

CHARLES. What? What are you saying?

NELL. I can't stay.

CHARLES. But we have an agreement!

NELL. Please, take it all back. The apartment, the money, I don't want anything.

CHARLES. You can't just leave!

NELL. I shan't embarrass you, sir. I'll slip away quietly. It'll be as though we never met.

CHARLES. But we have met! And you're my –

NELL. Charles, she could have been killed! The playhouse won't have me. They asked me to choose. But I have no choice. Because I can't have you.

CHARLES. You do have me.

NELL. I share you. And I can't do it any more.

CHARLES. You are more to me than all of them –

NELL. Am I? When you turn up with Louise – and take her to Newmarket? And York? And the playhouse? The playhouse, Charles! How am I different then?

CHARLES. I have obligations.

NELL. And I understand. Which is why I have to go.

CHARLES. Don't.

NELL. I have to.

CHARLES. I need you.

NELL. You don't.

CHARLES. You keep me afloat! Nell, they're about to mutiny. They want James gone and nothing I say will stop them. You're the only one who listens.

NELL. So make them listen!

CHARLES. They won't!

NELL. For God's sake, Charles, stand up for what you want! Their only role's to serve!

CHARLES. And they don't.

NELL. So why are they there? Why do you keep them?! Just be rid of them.

CHARLES. Parliament?

NELL. I don't know, you're the King. I have to go.

CHARLES. Don't go.

NELL. I must.

CHARLES. But I love you.

She stops and turns back to him. He's never said this before. Pause.

I love you, Nell.

NELL. You don't.

CHARLES. I love you.

NELL. You're just saying that.

CHARLES. I'm not. On my crown, on my life, I do. And Lord knows why! Because you're rude. And obstructive and – and far too frank. And damn it, you won't do as I ask, and you won't be told – and I'm the King of the bloody country. And you're – you. And you're truthful and that means everything. Nell, if it could just be you and me – I'd be a peasant, Nelly, if I could. I'd run away, go straight back to my oak tree. But this is my lot. And I need you with me. (*Pause.*) Both of you.

NELL *looks at him.*

NELL. How did you know?

CHARLES. I'm rather a veteran. Please stay. (*Beat.*) I love you.

NELL. Stop it.

CHARLES. I love you!

NELL. Shush.

CHARLES. I / love you!

NELL. They'll all hear!

CHARLES. And so they should. I LOVE HER! I LOVE HER! I LOVE NELL GWYNN! I LOVE NELL GWYNN!!

NELL. I LOVE CHARLES STUART!

Pause.

CHARLES. NELL GWYNN LOVES ME! NELL GWYNN LOVES ME!

Music.

Scene Seven

Charles Dissolves Parliament

CHARLES *arrives to address Parliament in full regalia. He holds the sceptre, wears the crown. He has clearly come to state his case. He addresses the assembled* POLITICIANS. ARLINGTON *is present.*

CHARLES. My Lords and Gentlemen, we are sensible of the extraordinary care you have taken, in these times of danger, for the preservation of our Person. We congratulate you on your success – for here we are. And, in return, we have brought you peace. Kept England safe and Christendom in repose. Led one United Kingdom.

And yet, gentlemen, the winds of dissent do shake these ancient walls. Let these words echo hereafter – no parliament can disinherit an heir. His Highness, James Stuart, Duke of York, is the rightful successor, elected by Holy God, and that which God sets down no man must put asunder – whether he be Catholic or not.

Do you suppose that one man could turn us about to Popery? To believe so is to damn us all as Godless. Is it not irreligious that we should dispossess a man of his right, because he differs in point of faith? Such prejudice only leads to war. And we will not accept counsel from those who expound this path.

The crown is not elective, gentlemen. Parliament is. We declare it our Royal will to dissolve this present Government. Gentlemen, take your leave. Go home.

The COURT *all leave.* ARLINGTON *goes to leave. He is a broken man.*

Arlington.

ARLINGTON. Sir.

CHARLES. You didn't think I'd do it, did you?

ARLINGTON. No, sir.

CHARLES. You underestimated me. Have you anything to say?

ARLINGTON. –

CHARLES. Where will you go?

ARLINGTON. I hardly know. (*Pause.*) Thank you. For everything. I… thank you.

He goes to leave. NELL, *who has arrived, speaks and stops him.*

NELL. Arlington.

CHARLES. Arlington is leaving.

NELL. Leaving? Isn't there a role for him in your new Court?

CHARLES. Nell, I want him gone.

ARLINGTON. Please, sir, listen to the woman.

NELL *shoots him a look.*

To the lady.

CHARLES. What role? Had you thought of one?

NELL. Yes.

ARLINGTON. Go on, Madam. The Treasury? Europe?

NELL. Spaniels.

ARLINGTON. Spaniels?

NELL. You could walk the dogs.

ARLINGTON. Walk the dogs? But there are nineteen of them!

NELL. Twenty-two.

CHARLES. Oliver Cromwell took us all by surprise and popped out triplets this morning, little bitch!

ARLINGTON. Sir.

CHARLES. It's your choice, Arley.

Pause.

ARLINGTON. Where are they?

NELL. In the parlour. And they're *very* excited. They haven't been walked for days.

He leaves.

Scene Eight

Meanwhile, Back at the Playhouse

DRYDEN *hasn't finished his play, so the actors are in a last-minute rehearsal for Etherege's* She Would if She Could. NED *plays Courtall,* HART *plays Freeman,* KYNASTON (*dressed as a lady*) *is waiting to enter and* NANCY *is learning the maid's part.* DRYDEN *sits at the side, scribbling miserably. Tensions are high.*

KILLIGREW. And again from the top, thank you, Mr Spiggett.

NED. 'Well, Frank, what is to be done today?'

HART. 'Faith, I think we must follow the old trade, eat well and prepare ourselves with a bottle or two of good burgundy, that our old acquaintance may look lovely in our eyes, for, for ought I see, there is no hopes of new.'

KILLIGREW. And enter Nancy.

NANCY enters from the side, walking sideways, staring out terrified at the imagined audience as she keeps her front entirely to them. She walks as she talks.

NANCY. 'Sir, there is a gentle/woman – '

KILLIGREW. Nancy, don't walk and talk at the same time. Make your entrance. Place yourself then say the line.

NANCY. Do I have to do it again?

KILLIGREW. This is a re-hearsal. Re. Hearse. And again. Enter servant.

She re-enters.

NANCY (*very quietly*). 'Sir, there is a / gentlewoman – '

KILLIGREW. Can't hear you.

NANCY. 'Sir, there is / a – '

KILLIGREW. Speak up!

NANCY (*shouting*). 'SIR, THERE IS A GENTLEWOMAN BELOW DESIRES TO SPEAK WITH YOU!' (*Makes a dramatic about-turn and walks off, facing the audience throughout.*)

HART. 'A gentlewoman? Ha! This may be some lucky adventure.'

Beat. The actors wait.

KILLIGREW. Nancy.

NANCY (*reappearing*). Sir?

KILLIGREW. Why did you leave the stage?

NANCY. I'd said my line.

KILLIGREW. What about your next line?

NANCY. I can come back on for that.

KILLIGREW. It's the same conversation.

NANCY. So do you want me to / stay?

KILLIGREW. Just say it! Say the damned line!

NANCY. What is it?

HART. 'She asked me if you were alone!'

NANCY (*mimicking* HART). 'She asked me if you were alone!'

She begins to exit. HART *catches her by the arm.*

HART. 'And did not you say aye?'

NANCY. 'I told her I would go see.'

HART. 'Go, go down quickly, and tell her I am here.'

The actors wait. No one moves.

KILLIGREW (*dangerously quietly*). Nancy.

NANCY. Sir?

KILLIGREW. That's your cue.

NANCY. I don't have any more lines, sir.

KILLIGREW. Your cue to leave. Let's do it again, shall we?
    And when you hear the word 'Go', you go! Understand?

NANCY. Yes, sir.

KYNASTON. I'm dying out here.

KILLIGREW. Mr Hart. From 'Go'.

    NANCY *goes to exit.*

    Not yet, you imbecile!

NANCY. But you said go!

KILLIGREW. From *his* 'Go'!

NANCY. Right.

KILLIGREW. Mr Hart, from your cue.

HART. 'Go – '

    NANCY *goes.*

KILLIGREW. Wait!

NANCY. But you said –

KILLIGREW. At the end of his line!

NANCY. Right.

KILLIGREW. Do it again!

HART. 'Go, go down quickly, and tell her I am here.'

> NANCY *checks nervously and then goes.*

> 'Enter!'

> *Enter* KYNASTON, *dramatically, as Mistress Sentry.*

> 'Mistress Sentry!'

KYNASTON. 'Your humble servant.' Now, about this entrance.

KILLIGREW. What about it? You just walk on.

KYNASTON. Just walk on?! Good God, anyone would think it were as simple as walking through a door. Look to Master Shakespeare. 'We have our exits and our entrances.' Don't underestimate the power of an entrance, sir. In this particular scene, Mistress Sentry will enter leading with her nose to reveal her interest in other people's business. Like so (*Demonstrates leading with his nose.*) *Commedia dell'Arte.* It's Continental, darling.

KILLIGREW. Can't you just walk through the door?

KYNASTON. Absolutely not. Tell me, what is the door made of?

KILLIGREW. What? Why?

KYNASTON. Because it makes every difference to Camelia.

NED. Who's Camelia?

KYNASTON. Camelia Sentry.

DRYDEN. Since when has she got a first name?

KILLIGREW. She's just a / servant.

KYNASTON. You see if the doorway is ash, fine. Beech, willow, even conifer, no problem. But if it is oak… Well. You see, what you don't know about Camelia is that once, at the tender age of eight and a half, she found herself imprisoned on a Spanish vessel in the middle of the North Atlantic –

KILLIGREW. Edward.

KYNASTON. – when a mob of filthy pirates took hold of her father's ship. Poor Camelia was left on her own in the hold –

KILLIGREW. Edward!

KYNASTON. – until, fashioning a coracle out of an oaken barrel with her very own dainty little hands, late one Tuesday night, she escaped and sailed the ocean under the stars, with just a piece of cheese and the ship's cook Ronaldo for company. And that is why, ever since, whenever young Camelia passes oak, she will remember that time and momentarily lose herself in the memory of the barrel under the stars.

KILLIGREW. Jesus Christ.

KYNASTON. Never underestimate the power of a backstory, Mr Killigrew. Acting is preparation. (*Shaking out as he counts down, ritualistically.*) Three, two, one – (*Posing.*) Camelia! There she is!

KILLIGREW. Enough. Enough! This is a disaster. Nancy doesn't know it, Kynaston's obsessed with a giant lump of wood, and… and…

HART. Say it.

Beat. They all stop. They know what's coming.

Say it! (*Pause.*) We can't do it without Nell.

Scene Nine

Royal Flush

We move forward in time, and find ourselves outside. Birds swoop, Spring has sprung. CHARLES *is playing Pall Mall* (*croquet*) *on the lawn with* NELL. NELL *takes a hit. She misses.*

CHARLES. Nell!

NELL. Hey – I hit it straight!

CHARLES. Of course you did, that's why it's gone off round the corner.

NELL. It was the wind! Unless you've weighted them – have you weighted them? You cheat!

CHARLES. There's nothing suspect about my balls, madam. Give me the mallet.

NELL (*handing it over*). I'm rather fond of your old balls.

CHARLES. Old? I fear the whole of me is getting old.

Game play continues as they talk.

James will destroy this when I'm gone.

NELL. You don't know that.

CHARLES. It's inevitable. He doesn't think! And Lord knows he won't be told.

NELL. It's your shot.

CHARLES. He will spend until there's nothing left, then what choice will he have but to recall Parliament. And once he does – they won't condone a Catholic. One almost wonders what's the point. The pendulum swings – a new king, a new cause, then round and round again. It makes me feel quite melancholy.

NELL. Who cares what happens next? You won't be here to see it.

CHARLES. Well, thank you for cheering me up. I'd like to be remembered well.

NELL. Why?

CHARLES. Because it matters.

NELL. No it doesn't.

CHARLES. 'Britain's finest actress.' You must want people to know.

NELL. Why? They never saw me. Why should I give a fig? It's only now that matters. It's no wonder I miss the playhouse.

CHARLES. What's it to do with the playhouse?

NELL. Cos that's all there is in a play. That moment.

CHARLES. Go on.

NELL. London could be burning down –

CHARLES. Not again.

NELL. Or the Thames could rise, or your mother's dead in the ground. But just for that moment, we're all there, us and the crowd, all of us together – and, just for that instant, it's all that exists. And it fills us. There. (*Pauses and witnesses it.*) And then it's gone. And it can never be again. And then – it's someone else's moment. But for us who were there, just for that time, it was perfect.

CHARLES. Come with me tonight.

NELL. I can't go back.

CHARLES. It's a comedy.

NELL. I'm taking Charlie to see the peacocks, he's rather fond of them.

CHARLES. You'll have to go sometime.

NELL. It's your turn.

    CHARLES *takes a shot.*

CHARLES. The things they said to you –

NELL. They can't take them back.

CHARLES. Nelly, they're actors – they're emotional. And you're a little too proud.

CHARLES *kisses her.*

You should think about it. Now give me some space – this will be a shot to remember.

She sneaks around behind him. He lines the ball up, and just as he's about to hit, she blows on the back of his neck (or some similar affectionate move) – and the ball goes off in the wrong direction.

Hey! Cheat!

NELL. What did I do?

CHARLES. Stop distracting me. Stand over there.

He hits the ball in.

And that is what you call a royal flush!

NELL. My turn.

CHARLES. It's sixteen–nil.

NELL. You know I like a challenge. I'm going to kick your royal behind.

CHARLES. I look forward to it.

NELL *turns away from him. As she lines the ball up, he grabs his chest – he has no voice to cry out.*

NELL. And you won't even see it coming. Set the shot, line it up. And –

She hits the ball, hole in one. He collapses.

Boom! It went in. It went in! Look at that, Charles!

She whips round to celebrate with him. CHARLES *is on the floor having an apoplectic fit.*

Charles!

CHARLES. I can't breathe.

NELL. No! (*Shouting.*) The King is ill! The King is ill! (*To* CHARLES.) Charlie.

CHARLES. Help me.

NELL. Help! Help!

ATTENDANTS *turn up*.

ATTENDANT. Call the physician!

NELL. He just collapsed.

ATTENDANT. Your Majesty?

NELL. Charles!

CHARLES (*fading*). My Nelly...

NELL (*to* CHARLES). Don't you talk like that –

ATTENDANT (*to another*). Get her out of here.

NELL. Get off me...

ATTENDANT. Take her away.

NELL. He needs me! (*As they're pulling her out*.) Charles!
   Charlie!

   *Exeunt. She is pulled away. He is carried out in the opposite
   direction.*

Scene Ten

As Charles Lies Dying

NELL *sits alone on a bench in a corridor. She is numb*. ROSE
arrives, walking with a crutch.

ROSE. Nell?

NELL. –

ROSE. No news?

   NELL *shakes her head*. ROSE *sits next to her. She unwraps
   a bun and offers it to* NELL.

   Here.

NELL. –

ROSE. It's got honey in it. Your favourite. You're wasting away. Here, just a morsel.

NELL eats a little bit.

Better?

NELL (*nods. Pauses*). How's my boy?

ROSE. Noisy. He's been building a fortress for the spaniels. Then I took him for a paddle in the moat.

NELL. He knows he's not allowed. Just like his father.

Pause.

ROSE. Nell, they've sent the priest in.

NELL didn't know. It hits her hard.

NELL. They won't let me near him. A French duke he's never met's allowed in. Every one of his courtiers. My own son. But not me.

ROSE. I didn't know you loved him.

They sit in silence. ROSE takes NELL's hand. NELL tries to keep it together. ARLINGTON passes with two ATTENDANTS.

Sir?

The ATTENDANTS pass, but ARLINGTON pauses and turns back to NELL. She meets his gaze. It's obvious that CHARLES is dead.

ARLINGTON. The King is dead, madam. Long live the King.

NELL (*through tears, numb*). Did he suffer?

ARLINGTON. He was quite peaceful.

ROSE. And did he say anything? At the end?

ARLINGTON doesn't answer.

Sir? (*Pause.*) What did he say?

ARLINGTON. He said… 'Don't let poor Nelly starve.'

A bell tolls.

Scene Eleven

Ensemble Again

NANCY *stands on stage, playing Valeria, opposite* NED, *who is waiting for his line in* DRYDEN*'s new play* Tyrranick Love. *The rest of the company are watching.* NANCY *is terrible. The situation is desperate.*

NANCY. 'Let me be just before I go away. Placenterous – '

NED. Placidius!

NANCY. 'Plass…'

KILLIGREW. Again.

NANCY. 'Before I go away – Preposterous – '

NED. Placidius!

NANCY. 'Plass… dous. I have vowed to… I have vowed to…'

KILLIGREW. Nancy. What has she vowed?

> NANCY *is frozen.*

> To be his wife! To be his wife! It is the crux of the play, remember! AGAIN! Perhaps with some semblance of feeling this time!

NANCY. 'Placidius! I have vowed to be your wife.'

KILLIGREW. YES!

NANCY. 'Take then my hand, 'tis yours while I have wife.'

KILLIGREW. LIFE!

NANCY. Life!

NED. That was better though.

KILLIGREW. No, it wasn't!

NANCY. You'll have to get someone else.

KILLIGREW. But there is no one else.

> NELL *walks in at the back.*

NED. What about –

NANCY (*seeing her*). Nell!

KILLIGREW. Nell? (*Turning round to see her.*) NELL!

NELL. Nan – you're in the play?!

KILLIGREW. When she remembers to come on.

NANCY. I hate it.

DRYDEN. We didn't know if you'd come back.

NELL. Nor did I. Sorry it took me so long.

KILLIGREW. And we are sorry – for your loss.

HART. Yes. We all are.

NELL. Thank you. What's this then?

NED. Mr Dryden's new play, *Tyrranick Love*.

DRYDEN. It's a tragedy.

KILLIGREW. Sort of.

DRYDEN. It's a tragedy… with jokes in. Not my idea.

KYNASTON. It's all right, they're not funny.

DRYDEN. It's about St Catherine.

NELL. Oh.

DRYDEN. I wrote it for you.

NELL. John.

DRYDEN. I hoped you might come back.

NANCY. It's been dead boring without you.

HART. None of the drama.

KYNASTON. It has been a little dull.

    NELL*'s taken aback by* KYNASTON*'s minor turnaround.*

DRYDEN. Please. Thomas, ask her back. She'd be marvellous.

KILLIGREW. But she hasn't been on for an age. And Nancy's
    persevering.

DRYDEN. Nancy's killing it! Sorry, but my play is expiring in front of my eyes like the Black Death!

KYNASTON. Too soon.

NANCY. Do it, please, I bloody hate acting.

NELL. It's been too long. I'd never / remember –

DRYDEN. Of course you'd remember. It's just acting.

KYNASTON. WHAT?!

NED. Please.

NELL (*looking to* KILLIGREW). I'm not sure it's up to me.

DRYDEN (*to* KILLIGREW). Say you'll have her back.

NELL. Mr Killigrew?

KILLIGREW. I don't know. It's a risk. Your voice won't be on form, who knows what the public'll make of it.

NELL. Sir. I'd work hard.

KILLIGREW. Would you?

   NELL *nods*.

   And you wouldn't be late? Or miss a rehearsal?

NELL. I promise.

HART. Sir, say yes.

NED. Please, sir.

NANCY. Say it, say it, for the love of Christopher Columbus, just ask her back!

KILLIGREW. Well. Would you come back?

NELL. Yes. Yes, absolutely.

   Pause. They all watch KILLIGREW *as he makes his decision.*

KILLIGREW. Then welcome back.

   Jubilation.

NELL. Wait – if I'm coming back – let me play a small part.

KILLIGREW. But you must play St Catherine – she's the lead.

DRYDEN. And she's got all the jokes.

NELL. I just need time. I'd like to learn again. And I'd like to play a serious part. I haven't done that before.

KILLIGREW. But we don't have a Catherine.

KYNASTON. Let me do it.

NELL. Let Kynaston do it.

KILLIGREW. What?

KYNASTON. WHAT?!

NELL. The King would have approved. I'm sure of it.

KILLIGREW (*to* KYNASTON). Well? Would you?

KYNASTON. I'll consider it. (*Beat*.) I've considered it. I'll do it!

NELL. You'll be superb.

KYNASTON. I'll be astonishing! St Catherine will be noble, transcendent, she will transform the theatrical landscape, she will recast the path of history, she will make grown men weep. I must prepare. I will set this part on fire! (*Exits*.)

NANCY. Does he know she burns to death?

DRYDEN. I don't think so, no.

KILLIGREW. Ned, you can tell him.

NED. What? Why me?

KILLIGREW. You can run faster than the rest of us.

NED. Oh dear God… (*Goes off in trepidation*.)

KILLIGREW. We'll begin tomorrow. Dryden, fetch Nell her role.

DRYDEN. Ah yes, I will just need to finish it.

KILLIGREW. You said you'd done it.

DRYDEN. I have. Except the epilogue.

KILLIGREW. Dryden!

DRYDEN. It's the hardest bit, the play's ended, I've said what I have to say but the bastards still want more.

NELL. Who speaks it?

DRYDEN. You should.

NELL. Then do you think... might I write it?

KILLIGREW. You?

DRYDEN. In character?

NELL. No. As myself. I've spent years speaking other people's words, but never my own. I'd like to speak. Just once. I don't know how many more I'll do.

DRYDEN. I'd be delighted for you to speak. If Mr Killigrew approves.

KILLIGREW. You're the writer.

DRYDEN. Well then.

NELL. Thank you.

DRYDEN. Good-oh. (*Pause.*) Better go and finish the middle bit then.

NELL. But you said –

KILLIGREW. Dryden?

DRYDEN (*going*). It's almost done, I just haven't quite written the words yet... (*Exits at speed.*)

KILLIGREW. Dryden! Come back here! (*Following him out.*)

KYNASTON (*reappearing*). Wardrobe!

NANCY. What?

KYNASTON. We are ready for our fitting. (*Exits.*)

NANCY (*to* NELL, *going*). You owe me.

HART *and* NELL *are left alone.* NELL *looks out into the empty theatre.*

NELL. I'd forgotten the smell of this place. Wood. Paint.

HART. Sweat.

NELL. Always sweat. It's hardly changed.

HART. I remember the first time you stood here.

NELL. I almost didn't come up. Imagine if I hadn't. Where I might be.

HART. Writing an epic with Aphra Behn?! Adventuring to the Indies?

NELL. Maybe. Or still in Cheapside.

HART. Or still in Cheapside.

NELL. You told me once to mine my own emotions. But nothing came. I thought I couldn't act.

HART. You could always act.

NELL. But I didn't… feel. Not really. I didn't know then what it was to love. Or to lose. (*Pause*.) When he died I felt like I'd been capsized. Sunk. It was like stones had filled me and I couldn't breathe. I don't know if I can find it again. That joy.

HART. There was a time I didn't think I would.

NELL. I'm sorry.

HART. And I. But you will. It's just time, Nell. And patience. You'll get it back. And until then, just do what all great actors have done since the Grecians trod the boards.

NELL. What's that?

HART. Fake it.

NELL. Fake it? No, I couldn't do that. At least, not on stage.

HART. Nell!

NELL. You were so sure I could do it. How did you know?

HART. Instinct. And mad faith. (*Pause*.) And love.

NELL. Thank you, Mr Hart. (*Remembering their early exercise*.) MR HART!

Scene Twelve

Epilogue

We are in the final moments of Tyrranick Love. *A Roman battle and then the final sequence.* NELL, *as Valeria, speaks to* HART (*Maximus*), NANCY (*Servant*) *and* NED (*Placidius*).

NELL. 'Let me be just before I go away.
    Placidius, I have vowed to be your wife;
    Take then my hand, 'tis yours while I have life.
    One moment here I must another's be;
    But this, Porphyrius, gives me back to thee.'

    NELL *pretends to stab herself twice, and then* NED *wrestles the dagger from her.*

NED. 'Help, help the princess, help!'

HART. 'What rage has urged this act, which thou hast done?'

NELL. 'I can no more, Porphyrius, my dear – '

NANCY. 'Alas, she raves, and thinks Porphyrius here.'

NELL. 'Porphyrius, do not swim before my sight;
    Stand still, and let me, let me aim aright!
    Stand still, but while thy poor Valeria dies,
    And sighs her soul into her lover's eyes.'

    NELL *'dies' and then* HART *pretends to stab himself – and then the other two stab themselves. Two* 'EXTRAS' *arrive with a stretcher and pick up the* 'dead' NELL. *When they get halfway across the stage she sits up and tells them to stop, in order for her to speak the epilogue.*

Hold! Are you mad? You damn'd, confounded dog!
I am to rise, and speak the epilogue.
(*Getting up.*) I come, kind gentlemen, strange news to tell ye;
I am the ghost of poor departed Nelly.
Sweet ladies, be not frighted; I'll be civil;
I'm what I was, a little harmless devil.
For, after death, we sprights have just such natures,
We had, for all the world, when human creatures;
And, therefore, I, that was an actress here,
Play all my tricks in hell, a goblin there.

Gallants, look to 't, you say there are no sprites;
But I'll come dance about your beds at nights;
And faith you'll be in a sweet kind of taking,
When I surprise you between sleep and waking.
To tell you true, I walk, because I die
Out of my calling, in a tragedy.
O poet, damn'd dull poet, who could prove
So senseless, to make Nelly die for love!
Nay, what's yet worse, to kill me in the prime
Of Easter-term, in tart and cheesecake time!
So, farewell, gentlemen, make haste to me,
I'm sure e're long to have your company.
As for my epitaph when I am gone,
I'll trust no poet, but will write my own:
'*Here Nelly lies, who, though she lived a Slattern,*
Yet died a Princess, acting in St Catherine.'

She stands and takes in the audience. She looks to
CHARLES*'s box, but it is empty. She gathers herself, then*
she lies down gracefully to join the rest of the COMPANY,
dead on stage. The crowd go mad for her. They stand and
take their bow.

The End.